CHILDREN'S ISSUES, LAWS AND PROGRAMS

WORKING WITH THE COURTS IN CHILD PROTECTION

CHILDREN'S ISSUES, LAWS AND PROGRAMS

Federal Programs for Troubled Youth
Killian Lucero (Editor)
2009. ISBN: 978-1-60692-318-4
2009. ISBN: 978-1-60876-701-4 (E-book)

Child Sexual Abuse: Pitfalls in the Substantiation Process
Anna Aprile, Cristina Ranzato, Melissa Rosa Rizzotto and Paola Facchin
2009. ISBN: 978-1-60741-427-8

National School Lunch Program Assessment
Manuel P. Borges (Editor)
2009. ISBN: 978-1-60692-972-8

Reading First Impact Study
Beth C. Games , Howard S. Bloom, James J. Kemple, Robin Tepper Jacob, Beth Boulay, Laurie Bozzi, Linda Caswell, Megan Horst, W. Carter Smith, Robert G. St.Pierre, Fatih Unlu, Corinne Herlihy and Pei Zhu
2009. ISBN: 978-1-60741-529-9

Diet Quality of American Young Children
Calvin G. Parker (Editor)
2010. ISBN: 978-1-60692-771-7

Diet Quality of American School-Age Children
Kelly B. Volkarsky (Editor)
2010. ISBN: 978-1-60692-776-2

Vulnerable and Disconnected Youth: Background and Policies
Dierk Neumann (Editor)
2010. ISBN: 978-1-60741-488-9

Foster Care and African-American Youth
Joanna Kaczmarek (Editor)
2010. ISBN: 978-1-60741-541-1

Preschool Children: Physical Activity, Behavioral Assessment and Developmental Challenges
Leone Colombo and Rachele Bianchi (Editors)
2010. ISBN: 978-1-60876-026-8

Child Development and Child Poverty
Anselm Fiedler and Isidor Kuester (Editors)
2010 ISBN: 978-1-60741-816-0

Child Labor in America
Ian C. Rivera and Natasha M. Howard (Editors)
2010 ISBN: 978-1-60876-769-4

Adam Walsh Child Protection and Safety Act: Analysis and Law
Terrell G. Sandoval (Editor)
2010 ISBN: 978-1-61668-808-0
2010 ISBN: 978-1-61668-878-3 (E-book)

Child Protection, the Courts and Social Workers
Terrance R. Langely (Editor)
2010 ISBN: 978-1-60741-279-3

When Abuse and Neglect Occur at Residential Treatment Facilities
Kirsten S. Madsen (Editor)
2010 ISBN: 978-1-60876-965-0
2010. ISBN: 978-1-61728-054-2 (E-book)

Child Abduction Resources
Melanie H. Wilson (Editor)
2010 ISBN: 978-1-61668-247-7

Working with the Courts in Child Protection
Raymond T. Devon (Editor)
2010 ISBN: 978-1-61668-303-0
2010 ISBN: 978-1-61668-426-6 (E-book)

Load Carriage in School Children: Epidemiology and Exercise Science
Youlian Hong (Editor)
2010. ISBN: 978-1-61668-622-2
2010. ISBN: 978-1-61728-081-8 (E-book)

Children's Social Competence: Theory and Intervention
Melissa L. Greene, Jo R. Hariton, Andrew L. Robins and Barbara L. Flye
2010. ISBN: 978-1-61668-861-5
2010. ISBN: 978-1-61728-640-7 (E-book)

CHILDREN'S ISSUES, LAWS AND PROGRAMS

WORKING WITH THE COURTS IN CHILD PROTECTION

RAYMOND T. DEVON
EDITOR

Nova Science Publishers, Inc.
New York

For permission to use material from this book please contact us:
Telephone 631-231-7269; Fax 631-231-8175
Web Site: http://www.novapublishers.com

LIBRARY OF CONGRESS CATALOGING-IN-PUBLICATION DATA

Available Upon Request

ISBN : 978-1-61668-303-0

Published by Nova Science Publishers, Inc. ✣ New York

CONTENTS

PREFACE

By having a thorough knowledge of this legal process and by working in partnership with the courts, child protective (CPS) caseworkers, and other professionals can work toward the safety, permanency, and well-being of children more effectively. This book, provides a basis for understanding court processes most relevant to child abuse and neglect cases. It may also be useful to other nonlegal professionals, such as those working in law enforcement, health care, mental health, and child advocacy, who wish to gain a better understanding of court processes.

Chapter 1 - The courts play a central role in making decisions regarding the protection of children who have been maltreated. Understanding this process is crucial for any professional involved in child protection. By having a thorough knowledge of this legal process and by working in partnership with the courts, child protective services (CPS) caseworkers and other professionals can work toward the safety, permanency, and well-being of children more effectively.

Child maltreatment cases are handled in a variety of courts. Thus, the rules and procedures that govern these cases may differ depending on the *type* of proceeding within which an allegation of abuse is brought, the laws governing the court involved, and the local practice in a particular court.

In recent years, a number of reforms have addressed the unique nature of child maltreatment and the special needs of its victims. Both legislative and judicial efforts have improved the ability and flexibility of the courts to respond to allegations of abuse or neglect. Courts now have more alternatives and resources with which to work when faced with a case where abuse or neglect has been established by the required burden of proof under State law.

Chapter 2 - State courts, including county and municipal courts, are responsible for resolving a wide variety of issues and do so increasingly in diverse ways. In addition to going to court for child abuse and neglect cases, child protective services (CPS) caseworkers often also must be involved in court proceedings for child support, domestic violence, criminal conduct, juvenile delinquency, child custody, mental health, and directly related proceedings such as termination of parental rights (TPR) and adoption. How courts are organized and how they divide their caseloads vary widely by State and even within a State. Thus, it is important for CPS caseworkers to know which courts hear which kinds of cases in their communities.

This chapter begins with an introduction to the concept of jurisdiction. The chapter continues with an overview of the juvenile court, then provides descriptions of other specialized courts. To set the stage for the later discussion of court processes, the chapter also reviews the general powers of the court, as well as the rights accorded to parents and children in judicial proceedings.

Chapter 3 - Children had little legal protection from maltreatment until the early 20th century when addressing child abuse and neglect became a component of the new juvenile court movement. Court practices varied, but generally were inadequate to meet the needs of abused and neglected children and their families. The identification of battered child syndrome in 1962 heightened public interest in child maltreatment and resulted in the passage of legislation in most States to enhance protections for children.[1]

As recently as the late 1 970s, it was common that the only people in the courtroom in child maltreatment cases were the caseworker, the judge, and sometimes the parents. Children rarely participated in the process and none of the parties, including child protective services (CPS), had legal representation. Nor were there Guardians ad Litem (GALs) or court-appointed special advocates (CASAs). The court's role was limited. If it found abuse or neglect, it would place the child in the custody of CPS, and that ended its responsibility. There were no case plans, no court reports, no periodic reviews, no reasonable efforts requirement, and no permanency planning.

Chapter 4 - Other than judges or attorneys, most people find court proceedings intimidating and confusing. Child protective services (CPS) caseworkers and families involved in juvenile court face the daunting task of understanding the court process, the roles of court personnel, the complex legal jargon, and the court's expectation of them. CPS caseworkers need to be competent in navigating the juvenile court process to achieve positive outcomes for children and families. This chapter discusses the juvenile court process and the responsibilities of child protection caseworkers, attorneys, and judges at each step of a family's involvement with the court. Exhibit 4-1 presents a flow chart of the juvenile court process. Because the process varies widely across jurisdictions, this flow chart illustrates one example of how a child maltreatment case might proceed.

Chapter 5- Conduct that rises to the level of child abuse or neglect may constitute a crime, depending on State law and the circumstances of the case; not all criminal acts, however, are prosecuted. Some prosecutors are less zealous than others, or they may believe that all but the most serious of intra-family offenses are best addressed in the juvenile court. Other reasons to forgo prosecution are that it may interfere with rehabilitating families or be traumatic for the children, particularly if they have to testify. Cases typically prosecuted include sex offenses or those that result in the death of, or serious injury to, a child.

Child protective services (CPS) caseworkers may have information about the family that is critical to the criminal court proceeding. Caseworkers always should determine whether either parent or any potential caretaker in a child abuse and neglect case has a criminal record or pending criminal charges. This information can inform a caseworker's assessment of potential risk to the child and enhance case planning and service coordination activities.

Chapter 6 - Families involved with child protective services (CPS) often face multiple problems and complex challenges, some of which require court involvement. Matters involving child maltreatment or juvenile delinquency typically are resolved in juvenile court. Other issues affecting families frequently are addressed in other court venues. CPS caseworkers who work with families struggling with divorce, domestic violence, and mental health problems may fi nd these families involved in other court processes. As well as understanding the juvenile court process, CPS caseworkers also should be familiar with other court hearings that affect families and case practice.

This chapter provides an overview of three types of court hearings that may involve CPS families— custody and divorce, domestic violence, and mental health hearings. The chapter also discusses suits against CPS caseworkers and agencies and Federal class actions against agencies.

Chapter 7 - Most child protective services (CPS) caseworkers are prepared to interview family members, to conduct home visits, to document cases, and to work with other social service providers. However, there is one component of casework practice that leaves some caseworkers anxious and ill-equipped— preparing for and conducting themselves in court. Simply knowing the different types of court hearings and mastering legal terminology do not demonstrate a caseworker's competence in juvenile court. Skillful courtroom presentation, well-documented court reports, and a collaborative style also are necessary to maximize constructive family, agency, and court outcomes. This chapter presents practical guidelines to help CPS caseworkers prepare themselves for going to court, to help them work with children who also may be called to testify, and to improve their working relationships with the judges.

Chapter 8 - Just as judges have power to initiate improvements in court practice and performance, they also can be formidable roadblocks to such improvements. Some judges may be intentional in their determination to continue operating in familiar ways; others simply may be unaware of alternatives, their power to make changes, or the resources that are available to inform and to support efforts to improve court operations. The ability of child protective services (CPS) and of individual caseworkers to improve the court process depends on their understanding judges and knowing how to work with them, to support them, and to provide them with the information and tools they need to do their job better. This chapter deals with measures agencies and individual caseworkers can pursue.

Chapter 9 - An integrated and comprehensive approach to the complex problems of families involved with child protective services (CPS) and the courts is critical to achieving safety and permanency for children. Evolving Federal child welfare legislation has prompted CPS and the courts to implement innovative policy and programmatic changes. T us, the pioneering efforts of court and child advocates have created a variety of inventive practices focused on accomplishing positive outcomes for families. This chapter provides an overview of the Child and Family Services Reviews (CFSRs) and the courts and information about best practices and model court programs existing throughout the country. It also provides information about the importance of judicial leadership in improving court practice.

This is an edited, reformatted and augmented version of a United States Department of Health and Human Services Administration for Children and Families Administration on Children, Youth and Families Children's Bureau Office on Child Abuse and neglect, Report Dated 2006.

Acknowledgments

Primary Author

The Honorable William G. Jones is a retired juvenile and family court judge who served for 25 years for the Mecklenburg County District Court hearing child abuse and neglect, termination of parental rights, and other family court cases. He has been a longtime member of the National Council of Juvenile and Family Court Judges and its Permanency Planning and Family Violence Departments. In Charlotte, North Carolina, Judge Jones was instrumental in the establishment of the Guardian and Litem Program, the Children's Law Center, a Supervised Exchange and Visitation Center, and the Family Court. He continues to sit as an emergency judge in North Carolina, serves on two court-appointed panels charged with monitoring compliance by child welfare agencies with U.S. District Court injunctions, and acts as a consultant to various communities and programs regarding children and families in the courts.

Contributor

H. Lien Bragg, M.S.W., is a former consultant with Caliber, an ICF International Company. She has over a decade of social service work experience. Ms. Bragg has served in a variety of victim and community service capacities, including providing technical assistance to State and local public child welfare and human service agencies regarding the intersection of domestic violence and child abuse and neglect.

Reviewers

Howard Davidson, American Bar Association Mark Hardin, American Bar Association

Beverly Heydon, Howard County, Maryland, Offi ce of Law

Katherine Pinto, Howard County, Maryland, Department of Social Services

The Honorable W. Stephen Rideout, Alexandria, Virginia, Juvenile and Domestic Relations District Court

Sarah Webster, Texas Department of Protective and Regulatory Services (retired)

Technical Advisory Panel

The following were members of the January 2001 Technical Advisory Panel for the User Report Series contract. ~ e organizations identifi ed refl ect each member's affi liation at that time.

Carolyn Abdullah
FRIENDS National Resource Center Washington, DC

Lien Bragg
American Public Human Services Association Washington, DC

Sgt. Richard Cage
Montgomery County Police Department Wheaton, MD

Diane DePanfilis, Ph.D.
University of Maryland at Baltimore School of Social Work
Baltimore, MD
Pauline Grant
Florida Department of Children and Families Jacksonville, FL

Jodi Hill
Connecticut Department of Children and Families Hartford, CT

Robert Ortega, Ph.D.
University of Michigan School of Social Work Ann Arbor, MI

Nancy Rawlings
Kentucky Cabinet for Families and Children Frankfort, KY

Barry Salovitz
Child Welfare Institute/National Resource Center on Child Maltreatment
Glenmont, NY

Sarah Webster
Texas Department of Protective and Regulatory Services
Austin, TX

Ron Zuskin
University of Maryland at Baltimore School of Social Work
Baltimore, MD

The following members subsequently were added to the Technical Advisory Panel:

William R. (Reyn) Archer III, M.D. Hill and Knowlton, Inc.
Washington, DC

David Popenoe, Ph.D. National Marriage Project Princeton, NJ

Bob Scholle
Independent Consultant Pittsburgh, PA

Brad Wilcox, Ph.D.
University of Virginia, Department of Sociology Charlottesville, VA

In: Working with the Courts in Child Protection ISBN: 978-1-61668-303-0
Editors: Raymond T. Devon

Chapter 1

PURPOSE AND OVERVIEW

The courts play a central role in making decisions regarding the protection of children who have been maltreated. Understanding this process is crucial for any professional involved in child protection. By having a thorough knowledge of this legal process and by working in partnership with the courts, child protective services (CPS) caseworkers and other professionals can work toward the safety, permanency, and well-being of children more effectively.

Child maltreatment cases are handled in a variety of courts. Thus, the rules and procedures that govern these cases may differ depending on the *type* of proceeding within which an allegation of abuse is brought, the laws governing the court involved, and the local practice in a particular court.

In recent years, a number of reforms have addressed the unique nature of child maltreatment and the special needs of its victims. Both legislative and judicial efforts have improved the ability and flexibility of the courts to respond to allegations of abuse or neglect. Courts now have more alternatives and resources with which to work when faced with a case where abuse or neglect has been established by the required burden of proof under State law.

This report provides the basic information needed by CPS caseworkers to work successfully with the courts. It introduces concepts and terminology associated with the courts, describes the key court processes, and presents practical information to help caseworkers prepare for what can be an overwhelming experience. The report describes:

- The general or common court system;
- The powers of the court and the rights of parents and children in child maltreatment cases;

- The interplay between child maltreatment legislation and caseworker practice;
- The juvenile court process;
- The criminal court process;
- Domestic relations and other court proceedings;
- The issues involved in going to court;
- The relationship between CPS caseworkers and the court;
- Court improvement and best practices.

Appendices to this report include a glossary, resource listings, and guidelines for CPS caseworkers for permanency and review hearings.

Various terms are used within the field and throughout communities to describe CPS agencies and caseworkers, including:

- CPS agency:
    - Department of Social Services
    - Child welfare agency
    - Social services
    - Family services
- CPS caseworker:
    - Caseworker
    - Social worker
    - Social caseworker
    - Worker

In many settings, there is little or no distinction among these terms. For the sake of clarity and ease of understanding, this report primarily uses "CPS" and "CPS caseworker."

One note of caution is necessary. On its own, this report cannot adequately prepare any professional, legal or non legal, to practice in the area of child protection. Consultation with a skilled legal specialist is *critical*, as is comprehensive training on working with the courts, particularly with respect to unique State laws and local practices.

In: Working with the Courts in Child Protection ISBN: 978-1-61668-303-0
Editors: Raymond T. Devon

Chapter 2

THE COURT SYSTEM AND CHILD PROTECTIONS

State courts, including county and municipal courts, are responsible for resolving a wide variety of issues and do so increasingly in diverse ways. In addition to going to court for child abuse and neglect cases, child protective services (CPS) caseworkers often also must be involved in court proceedings for child support, domestic violence, criminal conduct, juvenile delinquency, child custody, mental health, and directly related proceedings such as termination of parental rights (TPR) and adoption. How courts are organized and how they divide their caseloads vary widely by State and even within a State. Thus, it is important for CPS caseworkers to know which courts hear which kinds of cases in their communities.

This chapter begins with an introduction to the concept of jurisdiction. The chapter continues with an overview of the juvenile court, then provides descriptions of other specialized courts. To set the stage for the later discussion of court processes, the chapter also reviews the general powers of the court, as well as the rights accorded to parents and children in judicial proceedings.

JURISDICTION

To hear and to decide a case, a court must have jurisdiction or "authority" over that type of case, as specified by State law. The allegations of the petition initiating the case must satisfy the statutory criteria for cases of that type. The court must have jurisdiction over the parties against whom the case is brought, such as the parents of a child removed from the home. It is the judge's responsibility to decide at the outset whether the court has jurisdiction over the subject matter of the case and over the parties. Objections to jurisdiction, although infrequent in child abuse and neglect cases, can be complex and require CPS to have legal representation.

JUVENILE COURT

The juvenile court decides whether children have been victimized by maltreatment, as defined by State law. It then assumes responsibility for ordering services and monitors cases to ensure that its interventions are as beneficial and effective as possible.

The Focus of Juvenile Courts

The juvenile court—the earliest of the specialized courts—originated in Illinois in 1899. Initially, the juvenile court's primary focus was on delinquency (i.e., the commitment by youth of what would be crimes if they were adults) and status offenses (i.e., transgressions of children that would not be crimes if adults committed them). The emphasis was on the rehabilitation and reform of the youth who came before the court. Over time, the juvenile court concept spread rapidly to other States and expanded to include protecting children from child abuse and neglect.

The juvenile court operates according to the legal power of *parens patriae*. The *parens patriae* doctrine stipulates that the State has the legal authority to act as the guardian of children whose parents are unable to provide adequate protection or meet their needs sufficiently.

Today, juvenile court judges hear cases alleging child abuse and neglect, delinquency, and status offenses. Most also hear TPR cases and adoption matters. Some juvenile courts have responsibility for mental health commitment and admission hearings, abortion consent waivers for minors, and petitions for emancipation.

The organization and structure of juvenile courts vary widely from State to State and within States, depending on how State legislatures create their court systems and on the volume of cases in each jurisdiction. Some large communities have full-time courts dedicated to hearing just child abuse and neglect or delinquency cases, while others have one or more full-time courts that hear a mix of juvenile cases. Judges in smaller and rural communities regularly hear a variety of case types and commonly hear all the juvenile cases on the same docket with other types of cases.

How Juvenile Courts Are Different from Other Courts

Juvenile courts operate like other courts when deciding whether a child was abused or neglected or committed a delinquent act or a status offense. What is unique about juvenile courts is that they also make extensive use of experts, including CPS caseworkers, juvenile probation officers, psychologists, mental health professionals, physicians, domestic violence specialists, educators, child development specialists, foster parents, relative caretakers, and others. The court utilizes the expertise of these individuals to understand children and their families better, why events occurred that necessitated court intervention, and how to prevent recurrence. Juvenile courts attempt to look beyond individual and family deficits to understand the family and child as a whole. They aim to make well-informed decisions to address needs for housing, childcare, in-home services, domestic violence advocacy, mental health or substance abuse treatment, paternity establishment, child support, educational services, or employment. Also unique to the juvenile court, particularly in CPS cases, are the frequent review of parents and the assessment of agency performance.

Specialized Courts

Many communities are experimenting with "specialized" or "dedicated" courts that focus on particular areas, such as mental health, truancy, domestic violence, substance abuse, child support, and reentry. Specialized courts are designed to require treatment and services for the specific offense in addition to, or instead of, punishment, such as incarceration. These courts are more common in larger communities that have available funding. Three specialized courts that are particularly relevant to CPS cases are highlighted here.

Family Courts

Several States either have or are implementing "unified" or "coordinated" family courts that hear most, if not all, of the different types of cases having to do with children and families. Family courts are characterized by:

- Case management practices that expedite the resolution of cases;
- Specialized services;
- Coordination of all cases involving the same family, often before the same judge;
- Extensive use of alternative dispute resolution methodologies;
- Reduced court appearances;
- Enhanced training for judicial officers;
- A commitment to providing participants with good customer service.

Model Family Courts

Currently, there are 25 model family courts located throughout all the States and the District of Columbia. The National Council of Juvenile and Family Court Judges (NCJFCJ) has conducted extensive information dissemination, curriculum development, and training and technical assistance in support of the model courts process. Its nationally recognized Child Victims Act Model Courts Initiative works to improve juvenile and family court practices in child abuse and neglect cases nationwide.[1]

A "model court" is created when a lead judge in a juvenile court jurisdiction seeks to implement the principles of court reform. These were first formulated in the 1995 NCJFCJ publication *Resource Guidelines: Improving Court Practices in Child Abuse and Neglect Cases* (online at http://www.ncjfcj.org/images/stories/dept/ppcd/pdf/resguide.pdf). The model court teams identify impediments to the timeliness of court events and to the delivery of services for families with children in care and then design and implement court- and agency-based changes to address these barriers. Model courts receive ongoing technical assistance and training from the Permanency Planning for Children Department of NCJFCJ.

Family court cases are fundamentally different from criminal cases for several reasons. First, they involve intimate, interpersonal relationships and highly charged emotions that profoundly affect how the parties approach the litigation. Commonly, the courtroom battle is an extension of unresolved personal conflicts. The adversarial process only heightens the conflict. Second, they involve multiple claims, each with a unique set of issues and timetables for court action. Third, the litigation is ongoing. Any changes in the circumstances in the lives of the parents or children, changes in the financial circumstances, or noncompliance with support or visitation provisions of an order frequently require renewed litigation.

Where family courts have been established, they typically include the juvenile court and attempt to coordinate cases that arise there with cases on other dockets involving the same family. They also provide access to a variety of services, some of which may be valuable resources in child maltreatment cases (e.g., child waiting rooms with capable caretakers when parents need to be in court).

Drug Courts

Drug courts, an increasingly common specialized court, emphasize recovery from addiction, provide access to immediate treatment, and conduct frequent reviews to monitor abstinence, participation in treatment, and compliance with court orders. The reviews are a constructive and supportive group process in which each participant's performance is assessed in the drug court. While drug courts handle mostly criminal cases and require an underlying criminal conviction to mandate participation, the number of dependency, delinquency, and child custody drug courts is rising.

Drug courts, including criminal ones, are resources CPS should utilize whenever possible. Studies suggest that parental substance abuse is a contributing factor for between one-third and two-thirds of children involved with CPS.[2] Drug courts can facilitate access to treatment, which otherwise may not be available. Individuals with substance use disorders who access services through drug courts generally initiate treatment sooner, have lower rates of recidivism, and participate in treatment longer.[3]

Juvenile and Family Drug Courts

Recently, a number of jurisdictions have referred to the experiences of adult drug courts to determine how juvenile courts might adapt to the increasing population of substance abusing juveniles and parents. The result is the emergence of:

- **The juvenile drug court**—a drug court that focuses on juvenile delinquency matters and status offenses that involve juveniles who are substance abusers.[4]

- **The family drug court**—a drug court that deals with cases involving parental rights in which:
    - An adult is the litigant (i.e., any party to a lawsuit, which means plaintiff , defendant, petitioner, respondent, cross-complainant or cross-defendant, but not a witness or attorney);
    - The case comes before the court through either the criminal or civil process;
    - The case arises out of the substance abuse of a parent.[5]

FAMILY DRUG COURTS

As of December 31, 2004, there were 153 family drug courts in 33 States and the District of Columbia. A family drug court, also known as a family dependency treatment court, is a juvenile or family court docket in which selected abuse, neglect, and dependency cases are identified and treatment providers collaborate to provide safe homes for children while simultaneously providing drug and alcohol treatment and other support services to the parents.[6] Family drug courts typically operate within the general court organization in their respective jurisdiction. In most family drug courts, the judge, after consultation with attorneys, CPS, and treatment providers, will decide which cases to accept into the program. Once in the program, participants are subjected to frequent drug screenings and may appear more frequently before the judge, sometimes as often as once a week, to report on their progress with treatment.[7]

Juvenile and family drug courts provide immediate intervention in the lives of children and parents using drugs or those exposed to substance abuse through family members. They also provide a structure allowing for the ongoing, active participation and oversight of a judge. Common goals of juvenile drug courts include providing children with substance abuse treatment and services, offering constructive support to aid them in resisting further criminal activity, supporting them to perform well in school and to develop positive relationships in the community, and helping them to build skills that will aid in leading productive substance- and crime- free lives. The goals of family drug courts are similar, but also include helping parents become emotionally, financially, and personally self-sufficient and develop effective parenting skills.

POWERS OF THE COURT

Courts and judges often are viewed as possessing enormous power and influence. The power of the courts is ever changing, and the authority of judges varies considerably from State to State. Some courts exercise the authority to dictate to CPS where children should be placed, sometimes including specific foster homes. Other States are more prescriptive in their statutory laws about placement options for children in State custody and give less discretion and authority to the courts. CPS caseworkers who recognize and know how to access the powers of the court will find them advantageous to the resolution of their cases. This section describes seven different powers held by the court:

- Power to subpoena witnesses;
- Power to subpoena documents and records;
- Power to assist CPS investigations;
- Power to make negative "reasonable efforts" determinations;
- Power to hold individuals in contempt;
- Power to order treatment;
- Inherent power of the position.

This section also highlights how these powers can benefit casework practice and court processes.

Power to Subpoena Witnesses

Courts have the power to subpoena witnesses. A subpoena is a court order that directs a person to appear in court. Anyone who is properly served with a subpoena and who fails to appear as directed is subject to being held in contempt.

Courts also can compel a witness to testify, unless there is a constitutional right or a privilege that protects the witness from having to do so. The U.S. Constitution's Fifth Amendment privilege against self-incrimination is a protection that applies to criminal proceedings as well as to testimony in any other forum, including child abuse and neglect courts, if the testimony might be used against the witness in a future prosecution.

There are two types of immunity that the prosecuting attorney or, in some States, the judge may grant:

- **Use immunity**—bars the use of a witness's testimony and statements from being used directly or indirectly against that person in a subsequent trial. Future prosecution must be based on evidence independent of the immunized testimony or statements.

- **Transactional immunity**—bars any subsequent court action against the immunized person, regardless of the source of the evidence against that person.

Use immunity is generally preferred because it does not prevent prosecuting the person based on independently acquired evidence. For example, both parents are allegedly the only people present when their child is killed. The prosecutor may grant use immunity to the parent believed not to have participated in the actual murder to gain that parent's testimony against the other. If subsequent evidence is uncovered from an independent source that implicates the immunized parent (e.g., an eyewitness comes forward or a videotape of the incident is discovered), he can then be prosecuted. If transaction immunity had been granted, however, even with this subsequent evidence, the parent could not be charged. If either type of immunity is granted, the witness can be compelled to testify.

Depending on State law, witnesses who are doctors, clergy, lawyers, and mental health professionals may not be compelled to divulge confidential communications made to them by or about their clients. The content of these communications is privileged and cannot be disclosed without the express, informed consent of the client. These privileges encourage those seeking professional assistance to interact freely and openly with those professionals in order to maximize the benefits of their services and to eliminate fear of repercussions. Such privileges, however, may not apply if the client reveals child maltreatment. Under those circumstances, the professional may be required to make a report to CPS and to testify in court if a court proceeding results from the report. The court ultimately determines whether any claim of privilege applies. Any witness who refuses a court directive to provide testimony can be held in contempt and incarcerated until the testimony is given.

Power to Subpoena Documents and Records

Courts also have the power to issue a subpoena *duces tecum* (i.e., a court order requiring the release of specified documents or records). This subpoena commands a person to produce in court certain designated documents or records. For example, a court may require a hospital to provide its records on a child's care or compel a CPS caseworker to produce a case file or notes of conversations.

Power to Assist CPS Investigations

CPS caseworkers can face seemingly insurmountable barriers in their investigations of suspected child maltreatment. For example, parents are under no legal obligation to allow CPS to enter their homes to conduct an investigation. The Child Abuse Prevention and Treatment Act (CAPTA), as amended by the Keeping Children and Families Safe Act (P.L. 108– 36), requires a CPS worker to advise the individuals being investigated for child abuse or neglect of the complaints and allegations being made against them, but they must still protect the confidentiality rights of the person who reported the suspected abuse. (42 U.S.C. 5106a(b) (2) (A) (xviii)).

Obtaining formal documents and other information related to the alleged maltreatment, such as medical or school records, is also difficult. To assist CPS in obtaining information necessary to investigations, some States have granted courts the authority to order parents to allow CPS to examine and to interview their children and to compel others who have information relevant to a child maltreatment investigation to make that information available for CPS examination.

Power to Make a Negative "Reasonable Efforts" Determination

A court can find that CPS has failed to make "reasonable efforts" to:

- Avoid a child's removal from the home;
- Reunite a child with the family from which the child was removed;
- Secure an adoptive home or other permanent placement for a child.

A negative reasonable efforts finding can result in a court order preventing CPS from seeking reimbursement for the cost of that child's care or to report the finding to Federal and State oversight agencies.

"Reasonable" is a familiar term in the law, and determining what is reasonable is a familiar standard for judges. It is applied on a case-by-case basis to the particular needs of that child and family and the services necessary to meet those needs. (For more information on reasonable efforts, refer to the section on the Adoption and Safe Families Act (ASFA) in Chapter 3, *The Interplay Between Child Maltreatment Legislation and Caseworker Practice.*)

Power to Hold Individuals in Contempt

There are two types of contempt, civil and criminal. Civil contempt is the willful failure to do something that a court has ordered, such as refusing to testify when the court has found that no privilege applies or refusing to pay child support when there are ample funds to do so. Civil contempt is punishable by incarceration, which, in theory, can last until the witness relents and complies. Usually, however, a compromise is negotiated or one side relents before anyone is sent to jail.

Criminal contempt can be indirect or direct. Indirect contempt is a willful violation of a court's order. Examples of indirect contempt include a CPS caseworker's refusal to arrange for a particular evaluation or a parent's refusal to submit to paternity testing. Indirect criminal contempt requires advanced notice of the specific charge and a full hearing. Direct contempt occurs in the presence of the judge and usually involves some disruptive or disrespectful behavior, such as uttering an epithet when the judge announces an unfavorable decision. Direct criminal contempt is punishable immediately. Both direct and indirect criminal contempt can be punished by incarceration for a fixed time determined by statute, a fine, or both.

Power to Order Treatment

Some States specifically authorize courts to order parents to participate in mental health or substance abuse treatment. Whether or not the court has that power by statute, it does have the power to determine if the child should be removed from or returned to a parent, which may be conditioned on the parent's participation in treatment.

Inherent Power of the Position

One of the most significant judicial powers is not found in statutes or in case law; it is the power to gain the attention of others. Most of the professionals involved with child maltreatment respect the position and authority of the court and are responsive to judicial requests or inquiries. When a judge calls a meeting to address a particular issue or invites stakeholders in a child abuse or neglect case to a meeting, they usually attend. This is the power "to get people to the table." Of course, the outcome of such a meeting depends on the judge's leadership skills and the extent to which the attendees are willing and able to communicate effectively and to collaborate in achieving system improvements. (See Chapter 9, *Court Improvement and Best Practices* for more on judicial leadership.)

The Rights of Parents and Children in Child Maltreatment Cases

The court system accords both parents and children certain legal rights and entitlements, depending on the type of proceeding in which they are involved, including:

- The right to family integrity;
- The right to notice of the proceedings;
- The right to a hearing;
- The right to counsel;
- The right to a jury trial;
- The CAPTA requirement of a Guardian ad Litem or court-appointed special advocate;
- The entitlement to reasonable efforts.

Parents and children must not only be informed of their rights, but they also must understand the protections those rights afford them. Court representatives and CPS caseworkers can educate families about their rights and help them feel empowered in an otherwise intimidating process.

The Right to Family Integrity

Public policy has long recognized a right to family integrity, and there has been ample case law defending that right. The legal framework regarding the parent-child relationship balances the rights and responsibilities among parent, child, and State, as guided by Federal statutes. It has long been recognized that parents have a fundamental liberty interest, protected by the Constitution, to raise their children as they choose. This parent-child relationship grants certain rights, duties, and obligations to both parent and child, including the responsibility of the parent to protect the child's safety and well-being. If a parent, however, is unable or unwilling to meet this responsibility, the State has the power and authority to take action to protect a child from significant harm.[8]

A series of U.S. Supreme Court cases have defined when it is constitutional for the State to intervene in family life.[9] Although the Court has given parents great latitude in the upbringing and education of their children, it has held that the rights of parenthood and the family have limits and can be regulated in the interest of the public. The Court has further concluded that the State, as *parens patriae*, may restrict the parent's control by regulating or prohibiting the child's labor, by requiring school attendance, and by intervening in other ways to promote the child's wellbeing.[10]

In a recent case, the U.S. Supreme Court reaffirmed the right to family integrity in *Troxel v. Granville* when it said that parents' interest in the "care, custody, and control of their children is perhaps the oldest of fundamental liberty interests."[11] In *Troxel v. Granville*, the U.S. Supreme Court reviewed a Washington State statute authorizing grandparent visitation. The Court decided that the statute unconstitutionally infringed on *Granville's* fundamental liberty interest in raising her children free from State interference. This fundamental interest extends to a family's right to remain together.

As discussed in the next chapter, CAPTA is one of the primary pieces of Federal legislation guiding casework (See Chapter 3, *The Interplay Between Child Maltreatment Legislation and Caseworker Practice*), and it supports the right of family integrity through community-based grants that aim to strengthen families. Of course, this right is not absolute. A compelling State interest, such as the need to protect children from significant harm, will justify infringement on the right to family integrity.

The Right to Notice of the Proceedings

Parents or other custodians of a child have the right to "notice" of any petition filed regarding that child and to be notified of any hearing regarding that petition. The right to notice encompasses the right to be formally given the petition, which also must state what the parent has done or not done that makes court involvement necessary. The right to notice is a fundamental element of the constitutional right to due process. Due process specifies the right to be present in court, representation by an attorney, and procedures that are speedy, fair, and impartial. It applies to both parents, whether or not they are living together. Orders entered without notice are subject to being withdrawn.

Putative fathers (those identified as the biological parent, but whose paternity has not been legally established) also must be identified in the petition and be served. Their relationship to the child needs to be determined as early in the proceeding as possible by formal acknowledgment or by genetic testing. If paternity is established, these fathers or their families may become financial and placement resources for the child.

Petitions may be filed and emergency *ex parte* orders may be entered without advance notice to parents. *Ex parte* is defined as being on behalf of or involving only one party to a legal matter and in the absence of and usually without notice to the other party. For example, an emergency removal of a child from an unsafe home situation may be done through an *ex parte* order.

Action must be taken, however, to serve the parents with the petition and order as quickly as possible. Foster parents and kinship care providers also must be notified of pending court hearings and be given an opportunity to be heard during these proceedings. (For more information on *ex parte* communications, see Chapter 7, *Going to Court.*)

The Right to a Hearing

Another fundamental element of due process is the right to a hearing on the merits of a petition, including the right to cross-examine or to question any witness called by CPS, by the other parent, or on behalf of the child, as well as the right to present evidence on one's own behalf.

The Right to Counsel

Most States provide court-appointed lawyers for indigent parents in child maltreatment cases, but there is no Federal constitutional right to counsel in such cases. A constitutional right to counsel (i.e., every citizen's right to an attorney) does attach in some TPR cases, but not all.[12]

The quality of this representation varies widely among lawyers and courts. With the goal of improving quality, national, as well as many State and court, standards or guidelines exist for attorneys practicing juvenile and family law. Some jurisdictions also mandate training before appointing attorneys to child abuse and neglect proceedings. In fact, the amended CAPTA requires that attorneys representing children receive training that is "appropriate to [their] role."[13]

The Right to a Jury Trial

A few States grant parents the right to a jury trial in child maltreatment cases, but the right is usually "waived" or "voluntarily given up" by the parent. In criminal child maltreatment cases, by contrast, the U.S. Constitution gives adult defendants in every State a right to trial by jury.

The CAPTA requirement of a Guardian ad Litem or court-appointed special advocate

Children who allegedly have been maltreated are entitled to a Guardian ad Litem (GAL), who is an independent advocate for the children's best interest. States must comply with this requirement in order to satisfy CAPTA State Grant funding requirements. The GAL role may be fulfilled by the appointment of an attorney, a volunteer who is not an attorney, or both. Volunteers also may be called court-appointed special advocates (CASA). The volunteers often are professionals trained in other disciplines, such as nursing, psychology, or education. Responsibilities of the GAL or CASA include:

- Meeting the child;
- Exploring the facts of the case;
- Obtaining medical, educational, and other records;
- Determining the child's perspective and needs;
- Identifying appropriate services and resources;
- Monitoring the progress of the case;
- Promoting the child's interests.

Where both an attorney and a GAL are appointed, it is with the expectation that they will function as a team in performing those tasks and in advocating for the child, as well as in making the child's own views known to the court. These advocates can be valuable sources of knowledge and information and important allies when they and the CPS caseworker concur on how the case should be resolved.

In some States, an attorney usually is appointed as the child's GAL. Laws in some States require the GAL to advocate in the best interests of the child, even when contrary to the expressed wishes of the child. In other States, however, the GAL's advocacy may be guided more clearly by legal ethics that compel advocacy in support of a child's stated wishes. Although legal ethics may dictate that the attorney advocate the client's position zealously, there also is consideration in ethical rules for the common situation where certain clients (e.g., very young children) are considered incapable of possessing the judgment necessary to guide an attorney's actions. These situations likely will result in the GAL advocating what is believed to be in the child's best interest.

How children are represented in child maltreatment cases—whether by a lawyer, a volunteer GAL or CASA, or one of each—is a matter of State law or local practice. CPS caseworkers will want to know what model is used in their community and whether any advocates who are attorneys owe allegiance to the child's stated or best interest.

National Court Appointed Special Advocate Association

The National Court Appointed Special Advocate Association (NCASAA) promotes and supports volunteer advocacy in juvenile courts for children alleged to be maltreated. NCASAA provides money and technical assistance to start and expand programs, disseminates performance standards, produces training manuals and other publications, and trains program leaders and volunteers.

In addition to CAPTA's requirements of counsel or a GAL, minors who are parents also may be eligible, in some States, for a different type of GAL. This is nearly universal in civil cases, which include child maltreatment and TPR proceedings. The assignment is articulated in the States' Rules of Civil Procedure, most of which track the Federal rules, which state that minors are entitled to have a responsible adult function as a decision-maker for them in matters related to any litigation. The court appoints someone to fulfill this responsibility. If there is no conflict of interest between the roles of counsel for the minor parent and the GAL, the same person can be appointed to perform both functions. It is not required, however, nor is it required that the GAL be a lawyer.

The Entitlement to Reasonable Efforts

Except in certain aggravated circumstances, parents and children are entitled under the Adoption. Assistance and Child Welfare Act (P.L. 96–272) and ASFA (P.L. 105–89) to have State agencies make reasonable efforts to keep them together, or if a child has been removed from the family, to make reasonable efforts to reunify the family. ASFA also states that children who are not going to be reunited with their families are entitled to reasonable efforts by State agencies or departments to secure a permanent placement for them.

Federal law further requires that judges decide at each critical stage of an abuse or neglect case whether the agency has complied with the reasonable efforts requirement. The obligation to make reasonable efforts applies to CPS alone, not to the parents, any other individuals, or service providers.

"Reasonable efforts" is not defined in Federal law. Some States, however, have attempted to define it, and caseworkers will need to familiarize themselves with any definition in their State's statutes. Information about the application of reasonable efforts in a State's appellate court should be provided by the CPS agency's attorney to the head of the agency for dissemination to caseworkers and other pertinent staff, along with clarification of the decision's impact on their responsibilities.

End Notes

[1] National Council of Juvenile and Family Court Judges. (2003, October). *Child Victims Act Model Court Initiative* [On-line]. Available: http://www. pppncjfcj.org/html/childvic.html.

[2] U.S. Department of Health and Human Services, Administration for Children and Families (ACF). (1999). Blending perspectives and building common ground. A report to Congress on substance abuse and child protection [On-line]. Available: http://aspe.hhs. gov/sp/subabuse99/subabuse.htm.

[3] Harrell, A., & Goodman, A. (1999). *Review of specialized family drug courts: Key issues handling child abuse and neglect cases* [On-line]. Available: http:// www.ncjrs.org/pdffi les1/nij/grants/179281.pdf.

[4] U. S. Department of Justice, Office of Justice Programs (OJP). (1998). *Juvenile and family drug courts: An overview* (p. 3). Washington, DC: Author.

[5] U. S. Department of Justice, OJP. (1998).

[6] Huddleston, C. W, Freeman-Wilson, K., & Boone, D. L. (2004). *Painting the current picture: A national report card on drug courts and other problem solving courts in the United States* [On-line]. Available: http:// www.ndci.org/publications/paintingcurrentpicture. pdf.

[7] Cooper, C., & Bartlett, S. (1998). *Juvenile and family drug courts: Profile of program characteristics and implementation issues http:// www.ncjrs.org/html/bja/ familydrug/ welcome.html.*

[8] Goldman, J., & Salus, M. K. (2003). *A coordinated response to child abuse and neglect: The foundation for practice* http://www.childwelfare. gov/pubs/usermanuals/ foundation/ index. cfm.

[9] *Meyer v. Nebraska*, 262 U.S. 390 (1923); *Pierce v. Society of Sisters*, 268 U.S. 510 (1925); *Prince v. Massachusetts*, 321 U.S. 158 (1944).

[10] *Prince*, 321 U.S. at 166.

[11] *Troxel v. Granville,* 530 U.S. 57, 62 (2000); *Quilloin v. Walcott,* 434 U.S. 246, 255 (1978); *Smith v. Organization of Foster Families,* 431 U.S. 816, 862– 63 (1977).

[12] *Lassiter v. Department of Social Services,* 452 U.S. 18, 26–32 (1981).

[13] Keeping Children and Families Safe Act of 2003, Pub. L. No. 108–36, Title I, Section 114(b) (2003).

In: Working with the Courts in Child Protection ISBN: 978-1-61668-303-0
Editors: Raymond T. Devon

Chapter 3

THE INTERPLAY BETWEEN CHILD MALTREATMENT LEGISLATION AND CASEWORKER PRACTICE

Children had little legal protection from maltreatment until the early 20th century when addressing child abuse and neglect became a component of the new juvenile court movement. Court practices varied, but generally were inadequate to meet the needs of abused and neglected children and their families. The identification of battered child syndrome in 1962 heightened public interest in child maltreatment and resulted in the passage of legislation in most States to enhance protections for children.[1]

As recently as the late 1 970s, it was common that the only people in the courtroom in child maltreatment cases were the caseworker, the judge, and sometimes the parents. Children rarely participated in the process and none of the parties, including child protective services (CPS), had legal representation. Nor were there Guardians ad Litem (GALs) or court-appointed special advocates (CASAs). The court's role was limited. If it found abuse or neglect, it would place the child in the custody of CPS, and that ended its responsibility. There were no case plans, no court reports, no periodic reviews, no reasonable efforts requirement, and no permanency planning.

Since then, sweeping changes have occurred in the law, CPS practice, and the litigation of child maltreatment cases. Family dynamics and problems (e.g., AIDS, homelessness, substance abuse) have become more complex as well. These changes have increased the frequency of interaction between the courts and CPS dramatically and have transformed the nature of their relationship.

Therefore, it is imperative that CPS caseworkers understand the implications of significant legislation on successful outcomes for families.

The case example in Exhibit 3-1 illustrates a family experiencing multiple issues needing intervention. Following the case example are summaries of relevant legislation, including:

- The Child Abuse Prevention and Treatment Act;
- The Individuals with Disabilities Education Act;
- The Indian Child Welfare Act;
- The Adoption Assistance and Child Welfare Act;
- The Adoption and Safe Families Act;
- The Interstate Compact on the Placement of Children.

Following each summary is a discussion of how that legislation may be applicable in the case example.

THE CHILD ABUSE PREVENTION AND TREATMENT ACT

The first Federal legislation to address child maltreatment became law in 1974 with the passage of the Child Abuse Prevention and Treatment Act (CAPTA) (P.L. 93–247).[2] In return for Federal funding, CAPTA required that States adopt mandatory child abuse reporting laws, ensure the confidentiality of agency records and court proceedings, and appoint a GAL for every child in maltreatment proceedings in juvenile court. CAPTA has been reauthorized periodically and amended by Congress, most recently as part of the Keeping Children and Families Safe Act of 2003 (P.L. 108–36).

The recent amendment to CAPTA changed the confidentiality requirements so that States now are obligated to share confidential information with any agency or individual who has a statutory duty to protect children.[3] This amendment also contains language that allows States flexibility to determine State policies that permit public access to child abuse court proceedings.

- Caseworkers follow the definitions established by CAPTA and State laws to substantiate child abuse and neglect against Ms. Smith and Mr. Johnson. The condition of the home and the act of leaving three under-aged children without adult supervision for 3 days meet the threshold for substantiating neglect.

EXHIBIT 3-1. CASE EXAMPLE

April Smith is a 32-year-old mother of three children, aged 16 months, 4 years, and 12 years. CPS conducted an emergency removal of the three children due to allegations of severe neglect, inappropriate supervision, the sexual abuse of the 12-year-old child, and domestic violence. A CPS investigation concluded that the allegations possessed substantial evidence warranting ongoing CPS involvement and the filing of a petition to juvenile court for foster care placement.

The CPS petition contained the following information and allegations:

- The 16-month-old and two unrelated 7-year-old children were left at home for approximately 3 days in the care of the 12-year-old child without any adult supervision;
- The 4-year-old and 12-year-old children reported witnessing violent, physical attacks against Ms. Smith;
- The 12-year-old child reported that Robert Johnson had touched her inappropriately on three occasions;
- The 12-year-old attempted suicide, is failing academically in school, is suspected of having a learning disability, and was suspended from school on two occasions for fighting with peers;
- The rental home was littered with broken glass, animal and human feces, molding food, and hazardous electrical fi xtures;
- The domestic violence perpetrator, Mr. Johnson, is the biological father of Ms. Smith's 16-month-old and 4-year-old children, but Ms. Smith and Mr. Johnson are not married;
- Ms. Smith abuses alcohol and cocaine;
- Mr. Johnson also abuses alcohol and cocaine;
- Ms. Smith was employed by a cleaning service, but recently lost her job;
- Mr. Johnson is employed as a landscaper.

The initial hearing granted CPS temporary legal and physical custody of the three children. At the adjudication hearing, the court ordered that the children be placed in foster care, that CPS develop a case plan for reunification, and that Ms. Smith and Mr. Johnson cooperate with CPS in receiving services. (See Chapter 4, *The Juvenile Court Process*, for definitions of "initial hearing" and "adjudication hearing.")

The CPS caseworker assigned to the Smith family faced several issues:

- The siblings were not placed in the same foster home. While the 16-month-old and 4-year-old children were placed in the same foster home, the lack of available therapeutic foster homes or residential facilities prompted placement of the 12-year-old child in a temporary receiving shelter until approval was granted for placement into a therapeutic residential facility or home located in a neighboring State. There were no known relatives available for placement.
- The whereabouts of Eric Lequoi, the alleged biological father of the 12-year-old child, were unknown. Mr. Lequoi's last known whereabouts were with his family at a Native American reservation in Wyoming.
- Ms. Smith denied having a substance abuse problem and wanted to maintain her relationship with Mr. Johnson.
- Mr. Johnson refused to participate in substance abuse treatment, sexual off ender assessment, or a batterer intervention program and denied that he was the biological father of the 16-month-old child. Ms. Smith maintained that Mr. Johnson was the biological father of the 16-month-old and 4-year-old children.

Considerations and actions regarding this case and how existing legislation affects the provision of services are discussed throughout the remainder of this chapter.

The Individuals with Disabilities Education Act

Originally enacted in 1975, the Individuals with Disabilities Education Act (IDEA) (P.L. 94–142) entitles eligible children to education programs that meet their special needs. An Individual Education Plan (IEP) is developed for eligible children to identify their specific educational needs as well as strategies for meeting them. In its most recent reauthorization, CAPTA contains a provision that requires CPS to refer children under the age of three for evaluation of IDEA eligibility in substantiated cases of abuse or neglect.[4]

- The 12-year-old child's poor academic performance and possible learning disability are significant presenting problems. IDEA offers the CPS caseworker the opportunity to engage Ms. Smith in meeting the educational needs of her child and in coordinating services with the child's teacher and special education administrator. IDEA also provides access to individualized services that address the child's educational needs, as well as her emotional and mental difficulties. Through IDEA, CPS can demonstrate reasonable efforts to collaborate with external agencies to meet children's needs and to reunify families.

The Indian Child Welfare Act

The Indian Child Welfare Act (ICWA) (P.L. 95– 608) of 1978 requires specific protections to Native American children involved in CPS and juvenile court proceedings. If a child is affiliated with a tribal organization, the tribe has the right to intervene in proceedings or to petition to have the case transferred to tribal court.[5]

- Eric Lequoi, the alleged father of the 12-year-old child, is Native American. The CPS caseworker will need to locate Mr. Lequoi to establish paternity. If he is the child's biological father, the caseworker will need to determine whether he is a viable permanency option for the child or can provide child support and medical insurance. Once the paternity of the child is established, the caseworker will need to determine whether the child is entitled to the protections of ICWA.

The Adoption Assistance and Child Welfare act

The Adoption Assistance and Child Welfare Act (P.L. 96–272) of 1980 requires that CPS make reasonable efforts to avoid unnecessary removals of children from their homes and to reunify foster children with their families. "Reasonable efforts" means providing a parent with useful resources that enable them to protect the child, to provide a stable home environment, and to promote the child's well-being.

If the court finds that reasonable efforts have not been made, CPS funding from Federal and State sources may be reduced.

- In this case example, the requirements for bypassing reunification efforts are not met, so the caseworkers should assume that the goal is to reunify the children with their biological parent, Ms. Smith. (For more information on circumstances where reunification should not be the goal, see the next section on The Adoption and Safe Families Act, as well as Exhibit 4.2, Circumstances Under Which Reunification Is Not Attempted.) In order to meet the reasonable efforts requirement, the CPS caseworker must conduct a comprehensive and thorough family assessment to identify specific services that will address the issues prompting removal of the children. The CPS caseworker, for example, may recommend that a domestic violence specialist conduct a domestic violence assessment with Ms. Smith and that Mr. Johnson participate in a batterer intervention program.
- In this case, the court also may expect that the following services will be offered to demonstrate reasonable efforts:
    - A developmental or medical assessment of the children;
    - A child sexual abuse assessment of the 12- year-old;
    - A substance abuse assessment and treatment plan for Ms. Smith and Mr. Johnson;
    - Domestic violence counseling;
    - A parenting program;
    - Emergency benefits for the family (e.g., temporary shelter, groceries voucher);
    - Enrollment in the Temporary Assistance for Needy Families program;
    - Vocational rehabilitation services;
    - Parent and sibling visitation.
- Additionally, reasonable efforts require that services be available and accessible to Ms. Smith and Mr. Johnson. Thus, if transportation to substance abuse treatment or weekly urine screens is an issue, the CPS caseworker may want to provide transportation or bus tokens to them.

The Adoption and Safe Families Act

In 1997, Congress passed the Adoption and Safe Families Act (ASFA) (P.L. 105–89) in response to concerns that many children were remaining in foster care for long periods or experiencing multiple placements. The law requires timely permanency planning for children. Permanency for children involves either reunification with the biological parent, legal guardianship with a relative or caregiver, adoption, or an alternative planned permanent living arrangement. ASFA emphasizes that the child's safety is the paramount concern in any child maltreatment case.

In addition, ASFA addressed the lack of clarity regarding what constituted making "reasonable efforts" to keep families together. The legislation:

- Restricts the reasonable efforts requirement of attempting to keep families intact by permitting it to be waived under specified circumstances, such as severe or chronic maltreatment or the death of another child in the household due to maltreatment;
- Expands the reasonable efforts requirement to make it applicable to CPS efforts to secure permanent homes for children who will not be reunited with their families;
- Mandates a permanency hearing to occur no more than 12 months after a child is placed in foster care;
- Dictates, with some exceptions, that petitions for termination of parental rights need to be filed for children who have been in foster care for 15 of the previous 22 months;
- Includes several provisions to promote, to facilitate, to fund, and to support adoptive placements;
- Gives substitute care providers the right to receive notice of court hearings and the opportunity to be heard;
- Requires criminal record checks on all substitute care providers;
- Directs that compliance with these provisions and other performance standards be carefully monitored and enforced.[6]

ASFA has a significant impact on caseworker practice, guiding caseworkers through family reunification, the provision of services to the family, and alternative permanent placements, if necessary.

- Ms. Smith and Mr. Johnson abuse alcohol and cocaine, which exacerbates the incidence and severity of physical violence perpetrated by Mr. Johnson. Substance use disorder and domestic violence are commonly known to be chronic issues that typically require extensive time for successful treatment and resolution. ASFA requires that Ms. Smith and Mr. Johnson address and resolve their substance abuse and domestic violence issues in a shortened and restricted length of time. If Ms. Smith and Mr. Johnson cannot resolve their issues within 12 months, the CPS caseworker is faced with the possibility of making a recommendation at the permanency hearing that parental rights be terminated and the children be placed for adoption. The caseworker also could utilize concurrent planning, which seeks to reunify children with their birth families while, at the same time, establishing an alternative permanency plan if reunification cannot take place.[7] In either case, the CPS caseworker needs to be diligent and expeditious in engaging Ms. Smith and Mr. Johnson in services. It is equally important for the caseworker to ensure compliance with the court-ordered case plan. The caseworker also may collaborate with service providers to assist Ms. Smith and Mr. Johnson with addressing their issues in a timely manner.
- Establishing paternity is another critical piece of casework practice to prevent further delays in achieving permanency. If the permanency plan's goal is adoption, the children cannot be freed for adoption unless the parental rights of their biological parents are terminated. In this case, Mr. Johnson denies paternity of the 16-monthold child. The CPS caseworker must ascertain if Mr. Johnson's claims are true and, if so, begin proceedings to locate the biological father. Additionally, if the children remain in foster care placement, child support needs to be established and paid to the CPS agency by Ms. Smith and Mr. Johnson. If Ms. Smith and Mr. Johnson are separated, each parent will need a separate child support order. The CPS caseworker can utilize the Child Support Enforcement (CSE) office that is responsible by law for establishing and for enforcing paternity, child support, and medical insurance obligations for children in foster care. Collaboration with the CSE office is an example of the CPS caseworker's ability to demonstrate reasonable efforts to the courts and to ensure timely permanency for Ms. Smith's children.

The Interstate Compact on the Placement of Children

In addition to Federal legislation, the Interstate Compact on the Placement of Children (ICPC) also can play an important role in caseworker practice. ICPC is an agreement among all 50 States, the District of Columbia, and the U.S. Virgin Islands regarding placement (e.g., kinship care, adoption, foster care) across State lines. The placement must be approved by the ICPC offices of each of the affected States before it can occur.

- Due to the special needs of the 12-year-old consuming and can prolong the quest for child and the lack of an appropriate therapeutic permanency. Thus, the CPS caseworker will need foster care placement, an alternative foster to contact the State ICPC office immediately, care placement located in a neighboring State follow all ICPC requirements, and pursue timely was recommended. This process can be time completion of the ICPC process.

End Notes

[1] Kempe, C. H., Silverman, F., Steele, B., Droegmuller, W., & Silver, H. (1962). The battered-child syndrome. *Journal of the American Medical Association, 181,* 107–112.

[2] Child Abuse Prevention and Treatment Act of 1974, Pub. L. No. 93–247, 42 U.S.C. 5101, *et seq*. (1998).

[3] Keeping Children and Families Safe Act of 2003, Pub. L. No. 108–36, Title I, Section 114(b) (2003).

[4] Keeping Children and Families Safe Act of 2003, Pub. L. No. 108–36, Title I, Section 114(b) (2003).

[5] National Council of Juvenile and Family Court Judges. (2003a). *Indian Child Welfare Act checklists for juvenile and family court judges*. Reno, NV: Author; National Council of Juvenile and Family Court Judges. (2003b). Native American resource directory for juvenile and family court judges. *Technical Assistance Bulletin, 7*(4), 5.

[6] National Council of Juvenile and Family Court Judges. (2000a). Permanency planning and the permanency hearing. In *Adoptions and permanency guidelines: Improving court practice in child abuse and neglect cases* (pp. 9–22). Reno, NV: Author.

[7] DePanfilis, D., & Salus, M. K. (2003). *Child protective services: A guide for caseworkers* [On-line]. Available: http://www.childwelfare.gov/pubs/ usermanuals/cps/index.cfm.

In: Working with the Courts in Child Protection
Editors: Raymond T. Devon
ISBN: 978-1-61668-303-0

Chapter 4

THE JUVENILE COURT PROCESS

Other than judges or attorneys, most people find court proceedings intimidating and confusing. Child protective services (CPS) caseworkers and families involved in juvenile court face the daunting task of understanding the court process, the roles of court personnel, the complex legal jargon, and the court's expectation of them. CPS caseworkers need to be competent in navigating the juvenile court process to achieve positive outcomes for children and families. This chapter discusses the juvenile court process and the responsibilities of child protection caseworkers, attorneys, and judges at each step of a family's involvement with the court. Exhibit 4-1 presents a flow chart of the juvenile court process. Because the process varies widely across jurisdictions, this flow chart illustrates one example of how a child maltreatment case might proceed.

THE PETITION FOR REMOVAL

Cases of any type begin with the filing of an initial pleading with a court. A child protection proceeding is initiated by filing a petition. The petition usually will be captioned "In re Jane Doe," meaning it is brought regarding her. The State or county is the petitioner and the parents, caretakers, or child may be referred to as respondents. They are not "defendants" and the petition does not "charge" them with child abuse or neglect. The petition contains the essential elements of the conduct that is alleged to be child maltreatment. It does not need to contain all the facts known to the petitioner, but should include enough to establish the court's jurisdiction.

The decision to file a child maltreatment petition is made by the CPS caseworker and supervisor, often in consultation with the agency's lawyer. Most States allow only CPS to initiate child protection proceedings, but some also permit other public officials or even private citizens to do so. It is a complex and difficult decision that requires assessing the risk of harm to the child and weighing it against the distress caused by removal. The decision to file should always be based on safety considerations and not on how likely it is that the case can or cannot be won in court. As a result, child maltreatment petitions tend to concern children who are exposed to serious threats to their safety.

The requirements for reasonable efforts have resulted in more attempts to "remove the harm and not the child" by effectively addressing maltreatment without going to court. These attempts include diverting families to community-based programs and services, such as residential mental health treatment, substance abuse treatment combined with the placement of the child with a relative, housing subsidies, child care, or financial support; in-home services ranging from intensive family preservation to periodic monitoring; and ordering violent or sexually abusive adults out of the child's home.

Another important factor that CPS caseworkers and others in the court process, including service providers, must keep in mind is the importance of learning and respecting the cultural traditions and strengths of the families in which they intervene. Every effort must be made, either through written materials in the native language of the parents and child or by using certified interpreters, to ensure that CPS and the parents understand each other.

Content of Petitions

Petitions, or "complaints," alleging child maltreatment should be prepared by lawyers with the information provided by CPS caseworkers. These facts need to be conveyed in a manner that clearly describes what the parent or parents did or failed to do and how it affected the child. Together, the lawyer and the caseworker should construct a real-life story by identifying the characters, by describing the setting and the events, and by relating their impact on the child or other participants.

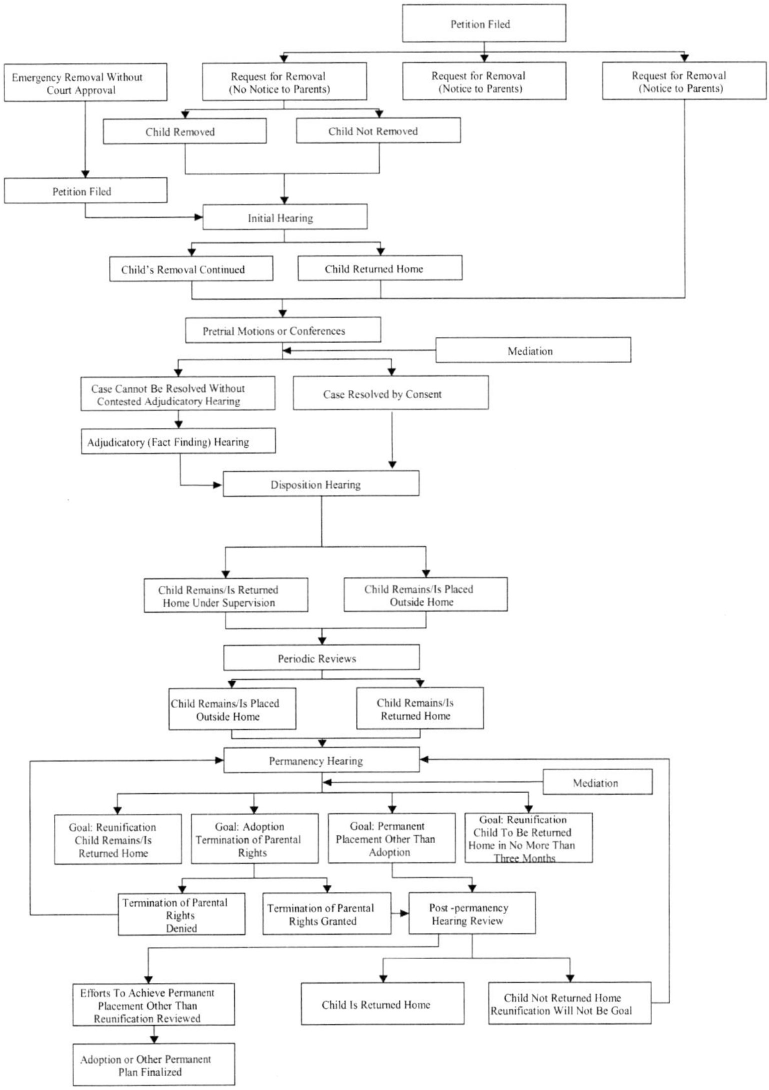

Exhibit 4-1. Juvenile Court Process Flow Chart

In documenting cases, caseworkers need to be careful to state only the facts and not legal conclusions. For example, the caseworker should write, "On January 1, 2003, Joe Smith hit his son Jack Smith, age 7, on the arm with a baseball bat, breaking the boy's arm," instead of "the father physically abused his son."

Lawyers' opinions and practices vary widely regarding whether a petition should be detailed or should recite only the facts essential to establishing jurisdiction. (See Chapter 2, *The Court System and Child Protection*, regarding jurisdiction.) The length of the petition also will vary depending on the complexity of a particular case and on local practice. Long petitions may be a useful guide for gathering and presenting evidence at trial. Care must be taken not to include any allegation in a petition that cannot be proven by evidence in court. Whether short or long, the petition must contain allegations of fact to support every element of the particular claim asserted. Otherwise, the court will dismiss the petition.

Filing and Serving Petitions

The CPS caseworker or attorneys representing CPS typically are responsible for delivering new petitions to the clerk of the juvenile court for filing. The clerk will file the case and give it a docket number and an initial hearing date. The caseworker should request a stamped copy of the petition.

Once a petition is filed, it needs to be served on the respondents. Serving a petition generally is accomplished by personally delivering to each respondent the petition, the summons, and the notice of hearing. Typically, the sheriff or another law enforcement officer is responsible for this act. In many States, service also can be made by registered or certified mail with a return receipt. In some communities, the papers may be served by the CPS caseworker. It can be difficult to serve persons whose whereabouts are unknown, so they will need to be served by following the State's alternative processes for providing notice of the petition, such as placing an ad in a newspaper. (See the section, "Termination of Parental Rights," later in this chapter for further discussion on this topic.)

Petitions and Removals

State and local practices regarding the filing of petitions, emergency removals, and prior authorization of removals by judicial officers are not governed by Federal law and vary widely between and within States. Ideally, no child should be removed from a family until after a petition is filed and the court has conducted a hearing at which the parents were present and had an opportunity to be heard. In reality, most removals are authorized by *ex parte* orders and the first hearing is conducted after the removal has occurred.

Petitions alleging maltreatment do not have to include a request that the child be removed. It sometimes may be useful to file a petition without asking for removal.

An example would be a case in which maltreatment is substantiated and removal does not appear necessary, but the parents are resistant to CPS intervention. The court may be convinced to exercise its powers of persuasion, or even coercion, to promote parental cooperation.

Where *ex parte* removal is requested, judges have the option of denying the request or of scheduling an initial hearing at which the issue of placement can be considered more fully. In making the decision whether to grant the application *ex parte*, the judge will determine the risk of harm to the child if removal is not authorized and what efforts CPS has made or could make to avoid removal or reduce the risk of harm.

When immediate removal of a child is dictated by emergency circumstances, a petition should be filed promptly and judicial approval for the removal obtained. The laws of some States set time limits for obtaining retroactive approval for the removal. Courts have procedures in place to ensure that CPS caseworkers have round-the-clock access to a judge with the expertise and authority to respond to requests for removal. If these procedures are not available or preferred by the court, a CPS caseworker needs to ensure that the timely filing of the petition occurs immediately after emergency removals.

In some jurisdictions, removals by police or CPS caseworkers are sometimes made without judicial authorization or any attempt to obtain it, even in non emergencies. This practice was condemned by the U.S. Court of Appeals for the Second Circuit, which held that "[I]t is unconstitutional for State officials to effect a child's removal on an 'emergency' basis where there is reasonable time safely to obtain judicial authorization consistent with the child's safety."[1] While this ruling may apply only to States within the Second

Circuit, it reminds practitioners of the importance of obtaining judicial authorization whenever possible.

Continuances, Adjournments, Postponements, and Delays

Continuances (postponements of a date of a trial, hearing, or other court appearance to a later date) or adjournments (temporary postponements of the proceedings of a case until a specified future time) should be avoided, if at all possible. They waste court time and inconvenience the parties, CPS caseworkers, attorneys, Guardian ad Litem (GAL) or court- appointed special advocate (CASA) volunteers, and witnesses. Typically, the impact of these delays is felt most acutely by the children and families involved. Most importantly, they delay resolution of the case and permanency for the child.

THE INITIAL HEARING

The first event in court after the filing of a petition is the initial hearing, known also as the preliminary protective hearing, shelter care hearing, detention hearing, emergency removal hearing, or temporary custody hearing. It occurs soon after the filing of the petition or the removal of the child from the home. The precise deadline for this hearing depends on State law. Ideally, it should occur on the first day following the filing of the petition, upon removal of the child, or as soon as possible thereafter.

The initial hearing is the most critical stage in the child abuse and neglect court process. Many important decisions are made and actions taken that chart the course for the remainder of the proceeding. At this hearing, the relationships between those involved in the process also are established, and the tone is set for their ongoing interactions. Too often, these hearings are brief and perfunctory, but to the extent that sufficient time is devoted to them to address the relevant issues thoroughly, initial hearings facilitate and expedite the resolution of the case.[2] From a caseworker's perspective, being ill-prepared, having incomplete information, or having a judge unfamiliar with family court proceedings typically lead to a poor initial hearing. Having thorough documentation, service plans, and an established positive relationship with the judge frequently lead to a good initial hearing.

The main purpose of the initial hearing is to determine whether the child should be placed in substitute care or remain with or be returned to the parents pending further proceedings. The critical issue is whether in- home services or other measures can be put in place to ensure the child's safety.

Parties to Be Present at Initial Hearings

Both parents, including any putative father, need to be notified of the hearing and be present. Extended family members who could become placement options also need to be identified as a part of this process. Issuing domestic violence protective, restraining, or similar orders directed to alleged abusers may be considered as an alternative to removing the child.

The child also should be present at the hearing unless it would be detrimental to the child's well-being. As an alternative, the judge may decide to meet with the child in chambers. Much can be learned from observing the interactions between a child and parent or other relatives, even in an artifi cial and stressful setting. In addition, the judge and others in the case who will not have ongoing contact with the child can meet, observe, and interact. This has the benefits of humanizing the process, emphasizing that the child is more than another name on another file, and underscoring that the child has real needs that require prompt resolution. Some courts welcome or even require a regularly updated photo of the child for the file.

Counsel should have been appointed for the parents at the time the petition was filed and should be present in advance of the hearing to talk with them and to prepare their presentation to the court. The GAL or CASA and any attorney for the child also should have been appointed and be prepared to proceed in advance of the initial hearing. Courts needs to have policies and procedures in place to ensure that these appointments are made and that the initial hearing is scheduled and conducted expeditiously.

Issues Addressed at the Initial Hearing

In addition to assessing the child's safety and making a placement decision, the court must make a reasonable efforts determination. Many courts require the filing of a reasonable efforts affidavit detailing the efforts that were made. Whether it is required or not, CPS caseworkers should be prepared to inform the court, preferably in writing, of the efforts they made to avoid removal and placement of the child or to explain the difficult or unusual circumstances that precluded the need to make such efforts.[3] Guidance for reasonable efforts and safety requirements for foster care placements are laid out in the U.S. Code as part of the State plan requirements of Title IV-E of the Social Security Act (42 U.S.C. 671(a)(15)).

Other issues that need to be addressed at the initial hearing include:

- The verification of any immediate needs the child or parents may have and determination of how they can be met;
- The appointment of counsel for the parents and of a GAL, CASA, or attorney for the child, if not previously made;
- The determination of whether the Indian Child Welfare Act is applicable;
- The determination of paternity of any putative father;
- The assessment of the need for mental health, substance abuse, medical, or other diagnostic tests for the parents and the child (sometimes these assessments cannot be initiated until after there has been an adjudication of child maltreatment);
- The identification and location of any absent parent or family member who is a potential placement option or source of emotional or financial support for the child or family;
- The resolution of child support;
- The provision of relevant records including criminal, medical, educational, and substance abuse or mental health treatment for parents and the child;
- The timing of visitation with parents and siblings if the child is placed outside the home;
- The appropriateness of the case for mediation if that service is available;
- The discovery (pretrial process that allows each party to obtain information relevant to the case from the other parties);
- The determination of the next court date.

The initial hearing should establish a supportive atmosphere in which parents are treated with dignity and respect. It is a process that should focus on understanding the problems the case presents and solving them as quickly as possible so the family can be reunited safely.

The judge also should explain to the parents:

- Their rights;
- The course that the case will take, including possible outcomes ranging from dismissal to termination of parental rights (TPR);
- The roles and responsibilities of each of the other participants;
- What will happen before the next hearing;
- The court's expectations of the parents.

The judge should promote a cooperative, problem- solving approach to resolving the case and control any conflict or hostility between the parties.[4] To the extent that the initial hearing may not conform to the process outlined above, CPS caseworkers are encouraged to do what they can to fill in the gaps for parents and to incorporate these approaches in their interactions with all participants. (See Chapter 7, *Going to Court*, for a discussion of judges' expectations for CPS caseworkers and how to work effectively with others.)

PRETRIAL CONFERENCES

Some courts use pretrial conferences, also known as settlement conferences, in child maltreatment cases. These conferences are opportunities for the parents, their attorneys, and the child's advocates to discuss a settlement in the form of stipulated, or agreed to, facts that would make a trial unnecessary. In courts where there are no formal pretrial conferences, these settlement negotiations often occur among attorneys by phone or at the courtroom and as late as right before the scheduled adjudication. The judge may or may not participate, depending on the jurisdiction and the nature of the case, and some judges will initiate such negotiations themselves.

Negotiated settlements can save time and money for courts, attorneys, parents, witnesses, and CPS. They also may avoid the trauma and acrimony that often result from contested adjudications. Additionally, they can expedite the development and implementation of the case plan, the terms of which are frequently included in the settlement.

MEDIATION

An increasing number of juvenile courts across the country are using mediation and other nonadvers arial dispute resolution methods, such as family group conferencing, to settle child maltreatment and TPR cases. The mediation process usually is called "dependency mediation" and is similar in many ways to settlement conferences, except that there is a skilled and trained mediator facilitating the discussion. Family group conferencing also utilizes a facilitator, but tries to involve the child's extended family more fully and encourages family members to craft their own plans for the support of the child and parent. When settlement conferences and mediation fail to produce agreement on the entire case, they nevertheless may produce agreement on some issues and at least shorten the time necessary for the adjudication.[5]

It is important, however, that provable allegations of significant child maltreatment not be negotiated away. CPS caseworkers need to participate in settlement discussions to ensure that the terms of the stipulations accurately reflect the seriousness of the maltreatment. A stipulation that the child was neglected, for example, provides no information about what actually happened. To support the development of an appropriate case plan, the critical facts of a case need to be included in the stipulations. These facts also enable participants in future proceedings to know exactly what issues necessitated court action and to measure progress.

Settlement discussions should include the child's advocates. The advocates and the CPS caseworker should ensure that the child's safety and needs are refl ected in the settlement. The court should require the recommendations of the child's GAL or CASA before it approves the agreement. Parents must not be coerced or be enticed to admit facts that they deny. Before accepting any settlement, the court must ask that the parents be certain that they have entered into the agreement freely and voluntarily and with a full understanding of the potential consequences and rights they have waived by doing so.

Discovery

Discovery is a pretrial process that allows each party to obtain information relevant to the case from the other parties. It is intended to avoid "trial by ambush," to narrow the contested issues, and to expedite settlement.

Discovery in child maltreatment cases usually involves the parents' and child's attorneys asking CPS for its records. In most States, they are entitled to those records. While details of the initial and investigative reports are revealed, the name of the reporter is not. CPS may not be able to look at certain records from other sources, such as mental health evaluations or substance abuse treatment records that carry their own confidentiality protections. Such records, however, usually can be obtained by other means. Records from a private practitioner may be obtained through a subpoena *duces tecum* (an order requiring a person to produce for the court specified documents or records). State agency records can be obtained by submitting a Freedom of Information Act request.

Other forms of discovery also are available in some States and jurisdictions. These include:

- Interrogatories or written questions that need to be answered under oath within a specified time frame;
- Requests for admissions that are deemed admitted if not denied under oath by a specific date;
- Depositions or transcribed oral examinations under oath.

The Adjudication Hearing

If the case is not settled by agreement of the parties, it will go to adjudication. Once the petition is filed, the court schedules an adjudication hearing (also known as the "fact-finding hearing" or "jurisdictional hearing"). At the adjudication hearing, the court decides whether CPS can prove the allegations in its petition. The CPS attorney will present evidence through the testimony of the CPS caseworker, law enforcement officers, or other witnesses, including any experts. Documents such as medical records or photographs also may be entered into evidence. The attorneys for the parents and the child will have the right to question or to cross-examine the witnesses and to present evidence. The parents may testify, as may other family members or neighbors who have knowledge of the facts alleged in the petition or of the care the parents provided their children.

Parent Testimony

Because child maltreatment cases in juvenile court are civil as opposed to criminal, the parents do not enjoy the right against self-incrimination contained in the Fifth Amendment to the U.S. Constitution. Therefore, they can be called to testify by CPS, the other parent, or the GAL. They still can "take the Fifth," however, and refuse to testify on the grounds that their answers may incriminate them.

In a civil case, a refusal to testify can be weighed against the witness. This issue surfaces when a parent is charged with a crime arising from the same underlying facts as the child maltreatment case in juvenile court. Criminal prosecutions, particularly complex ones like child sexual abuse, usually are not resolved until after the adjudication of the child maltreatment case. Thus, a parent who is called to testify in a juvenile court maltreatment case and who is facing criminal charges may refuse to testify to avoid having her testimony used against her in the subsequent criminal prosecution. The parent's lawyer may not call her to testify for the same reason. In some courts, parents may be granted "immunity" whereby judges can order that the statements by the parents in juvenile court cannot be used against them in other court proceedings. For more on immunity, see Chapter 2, *The Court System and Child Protection*.

Burden of Proof

CPS holds the burden of proof, and its attorney needs to present enough evidence to convince the judge that the maltreatment of the child alleged in the petition occurred. The burden of proof is either the greater weight (or preponderance) of the evidence or clear and convincing evidence, depending on the State. In determining whether the burden of proof has been met, the judge will take into account the quantity, quality, credibility, and convincing force of the evidence.

If the judge determines that CPS has met its burden, that determination justifies continuing CPS intervention and further court involvement. On the other hand, if the judge determines that the evidence presented by CPS fails to satisfy the burden of proof, the case will be dismissed, and CPS will have no authority to continue its involvement with the family without the family's consent.

Order

At the conclusion of an adjudication in favor of CPS (whether it is by agreement or after a contested hearing), the judge needs to enter an order finding specific facts regarding the child's maltreatment and the problems that must be resolved before the child can return home safely. Other issues to be addressed include whether CPS has made reasonable efforts to avoid placement or to achieve reunification, the child's placement, all incomplete or unresolved issues from the initial hearing, and the disposition hearing date.

The Disposition Hearing

At the disposition hearing, the court decides whether the child needs help from the court and, if so, what services will be ordered. For example, the court may enter an order that mandates counseling and rehabilitative services. The court also may enter orders providing for out-of-home placements or visitation schedules or for controlling the conduct of the parent. It also can order CPS to conduct follow-up visits with the family to ensure the child's protection. Essentially, the disposition hearing determines what will be required to resolve the problems that led to CPS intervention.

Te rules of evidence are relaxed in disposition hearings, and they are generally less formal than adjudications, although witnesses sometimes testify and are cross- examined. While the disposition hearing is sometimes held on the same day as the adjudication hearing, the National Council of Juvenile and Family Court Judges recommends that the disposition hearing be separate and follow the adjudication within 30 days.[6]

Court Report

CPS must prepare a disposition court report and present it to the court, the counsel for all parties, and any GAL or CASA at least 7 calendar days prior to the hearing or by the time specified in any local court rules. The court report should:

- Outline the history of CPS involvement with the child and family including identification of the current placement as well as all prior placements;
- Specify the reasonable efforts made to avoid placement and, if the child was placed, to achieve reunification;
- Identify and evaluate placement options;
- Update the status of any unresolved issues from the initial or adjudication hearings;
- Attach the case plan and any relevant evaluations, assessments, or reports (medical, psychological, psychiatric, developmental, or educational) related to the child or parents;
- Make other appropriate recommendations for court action.

The GAL or CASA also should prepare and distribute a court report in the same manner, addressing the same issues.

The Case Plan

Before the disposition hearing, CPS should confer with the parents and develop with them a case plan that identifies the problems that led to CPS involvement with the family and are specified in the adjudication order.[7] The case plan will state the goal for the child's permanent placement. When the goal is reunification, which it usually is at this stage of the proceedings, the case plan will:

- Identify the actions to be taken and the behavioral improvements to be achieved by the parents;
- Specify the services to be provided by CPS to support the parents in eliminating or in alleviating the identified problems;

- Set forth the time frame for completion of each component of the case plan;
- Articulate objective, measurable criteria for determining whether the necessary improvements have been achieved;
- Identify any special needs of the child and the proposed strategies and services for addressing those needs.

If inadequacies in parenting must be addressed, the case plan should identify the specific problem behavior, spell out how the behavior must change, and suggest some way of determining whether the desired change has been accomplished. For example, if a parent disciplines a 6-month-old infant for continuing to cry after being told to stop, the desired change would be that the parent learns about developmentally appropriate behavior and can demonstrate reasonable expectations of behavior by a child of that age. The mere requirement that a parent complete a parenting course would not be sufficient because course completion does not necessarily result in improved parenting skills.

Case plans should be tailored to the facts and circumstances of each case. A template for the case plan is useful, but "boilerplate" statements of needs and services to meet those needs are not acceptable.

In some States, TPR is a dispositional option, used only in the most severe and unresolvable circumstances, such as when adoption is clearly the long-term plan for the child's placement. More commonly, a plan to pursue TPR and adoption will involve separate court proceedings.

In some States, the court must approve the case plan. In all States, the plan must be discussed and refined at the disposition hearing, and any disagreements regarding its terms must be resolved. The case plan is the blueprint for permanency.

The Placement Decision

Placement is the key issue at the disposition hearing. The child can be:

- Left with or returned to the parents, usually under CPS supervision;
- Kept in an existing placement;
- Moved to a new placement;

- Placed in substitute care for the first time if removal was not ordered previously.

The option that the court chooses will depend on the circumstances of the case, principally the risk of harm to the child in the home and the possibilities for reducing that risk to a safe level. The options for placement will depend on the needs of the child and include:

- Either or both parents;
- The extended family or kinship care;
- Foster care;
- A group home or institutional care.[8]

As a part of its reasonable efforts inquiry, the court needs to scrutinize carefully any CPS recommendation that the child be placed outside the home. The caseworker making that recommendation always should be prepared to discuss why the child cannot be maintained safely in the home through the provision of in-home services, a restraining order prohibiting contact by the abusive parent, close supervision, or other means. If the recommendation is foster care, the caseworker also should be prepared to say why it is preferable to placement with any available family member.

Both CPS and the court should take care to ensure that the placement is supportive of the CPS plan for reunification of the child with the family and is otherwise appropriate to the needs of the child. Where feasible, sibling groups should be placed together. Ideally, the child's ethnic heritage, cultural identity, language, religion, or special diet, if any, should be accommodated without causing any delay in the child's placement. The placement should be in close geographic proximity to the child's school, family, and any siblings who may be placed elsewhere, if possible.

Review Hearings

Review hearings are the next stage of a continuing process that begins with the initial hearing and continues through adjudication and disposition. The review hearing is an opportunity to evaluate the progress that has been made toward completing the case plan and any court orders and to revise the plan as needed. If no progress has been made, and none seems likely, it is a chance to change the goal of the plan completely. Review hearings should guide the case to permanency for the child. Unless a permanent placement is accomplished on or before the date of the permanency hearing, the court must continue to review the case periodically.

Review Hearing Report

CPS caseworkers must prepare a court report for each review hearing that includes or is accompanied by a reasonable efforts affidavit detailing what has been done to achieve the permanency plan. Like the disposition report, the report should be delivered to the court, the counsel for all parties, and any GAL or CASA at least 7 calendar days prior to the hearing or by the time specified in any local court rules. The GAL or CASA also needs to prepare and distribute a court report in the same manner. The court report should update the disposition hearing report and also should include:

- Whether the case plan is on target;
- Whether the child's physical, emotional, and mental health needs are being met;
- Whether progress has been made toward achieving the case plan's objectives;
- What reasonable efforts were made to achieve reunification;
- Whether the child should be returned home and, if not, why;
- What remains to be accomplished before reunification can occur;
- What timetable has been established for returning the child home;
- Whether and how the case plan should be modified.

These inquiries are the essential issues to be addressed at the review hearing. The court also should consider any lingering issues from previous hearings or orders; modify child support, visitation, and other matters as needed; and set the date for the next hearing, if one is necessary.

Timing of Review Hearings

Federal law, through Title IV-E of the Social Security Act (42 U.S .C. 675(5) (B)), requires that States make provision for cases to be reviewed at least every 6 months after the child is placed in substitute care. Many States' laws also require court reviews, sometimes more frequently than Federal law dictates. The review requirement of the Adoption Assistance and Child Welfare Act (P.L. 96–272) also can be satisfied by internal CPS teams or citizen review boards.

The National Council of Juvenile and Family Court Judges encourages judges to schedule reviews more frequently than the law requires.[9] They may do so to expedite resolution of the case, to address an unresolved issue, to monitor parent or agency compliance with a court directive, or to respond to a party's motion. These extra reviews can be burdensome to the CPS caseworker and other participants, but they also can aid in moving the case toward resolution more quickly. CPS caseworkers who establish a reputation for making diligent efforts to implement case plans, for supporting the parents and child, and for pursuing permanency expeditiously will earn the trust and confidence of the judge. For these caseworkers, additional reviews are less likely to be scheduled. For more information on this topic, see Appendix D, *Guidelines for Child Protective Services Caseworkers for Permanency and Review Hearings*.

THE PERMANENCY HEARING

Review hearings are intended primarily to monitor compliance with the case plan, adjust the plan as necessary, and ensure that the case is progressing toward resolution. The permanency hearing is fundamentally different as it is the point at which a definitive decision is made about the child's permanent placement. ASFA requires that the permanency hearing occur no later than 12 months from the date the child is considered to have entered foster care.[10]

The Placement Decision

The options for permanent placement include:

- Returning the child home;
- Returning the child home by a specific date (no more than 3 months later), provided the court finds from the evidence that the parents are making signifi cant progress toward completing the case plan;

- Terminating parental rights, if necessary, and permitting adoption by a relative, foster parent, or other nonrelative;
- Granting legal guardianship;
- Permanently placing the child with a relative, foster parent, or other nonrelative;
- Providing another specified permanent living arrangement if the court documents and finds that there is a compelling reason why it would not be in the best interests of the child to proceed with one of the other options.[11]

In making the determination about the permanent placement of the child, the court must weigh which option is in the child's best interest.[12] In some cases, concurrent planning may be pursued. Under concurrent planning, an alternative, permanent placement is developed at the same time as the family reunification is attempted. With this approach, the child can then be moved quickly to a stable home if reunification with the birth family cannot take place.

Permanency Hearing Reports

To prevent miscommunication between the agencies and the courts, CPS caseworkers should submit a detailed report to the court discussing the preferred permanent placement option, the reasons for that preference, and each of the potential alternatives. This report should be distributed at least 7 calendar days in advance of the permanency hearing and in the same manner and to the same people as the disposition and review hearing reports. The report should be accompanied by a reasonable efforts report in affidavit form to aid the court in its reasonable efforts determination.

Timing of Permanency Hearings

In some cases, the permanency hearing is the last stage of child maltreatment litigation. It determines whether the final plan will be to reunite the child and parent or to pursue an alternative, permanent home. It is a more formal hearing than reviews. If it is contested, witnesses may be called to testify and to be cross-examined. Some cases, however, may never have a permanency hearing because the children are reunited with their families after brief stays in foster care, while other cases proceed directly to the TPR hearing.

Exhibit 4-2. Circumstances under Which Reunification Is Not Attempted

ASFA provides that under some circumstances reunification should not be the goal:

- A parent has aided, attempted, conspired, solicited, or committed the murder or voluntary manslaughter of another of his or her children;
- A parent has committed a felony assault resulting in serious bodily injury to the child or another of the parent's children;
- A final decision is being made regarding an involuntary TPR to a sibling;
- Other circumstances under which efforts to preserve or to reunify the family are inconsistent with the child's permanency plan, which holds the child's health and safety as paramount.[13]

The permanency hearing usually is held after 1 year. However, if it becomes readily apparent earlier that a reunification plan will not be successful, the permanency hearing should be scheduled as soon as possible.

As presented in Exhibit 4-2, ASFA specifies circumstances under which reunification should not be the goal and in which reasonable efforts to reunify are, therefore, not necessary. ASFA also allows States to specify additional aggravated circumstances.[14] The agency's lawyers should ensure that CPS caseworkers are aware of what those are in their respective States. Whenever the court finds aggravated circumstances, ASFA requires that a permanency hearing be held within 30 days.

Termination of Parental Rights

The 14th Amendment to the U.S. Constitution protects the fundamental liberty interest of natural parents in the care, custody, and management of their children. This protection does not disappear simply because they have not been model parents or have lost custody of a child temporarily.[15] Because the stakes are so high, TPR hearings are the most formal, longest, and frequently appealed of all child maltreatment proceedings. TPR hearings also may be called "permanent commitment," "severance," or "guardianship with the power to consent to adoption."

Grounds for Termination of Parental Rights

The grounds for TPR are specified in the statutes of each State, and CPS caseworkers are advised to familiarize themselves with these. ASFA requires that filing for TPR must be instituted when:

- A child of any age has been in foster care for 15 of the most recent 22 months, unless exceptions apply;
- The child is an abandoned infant;
- The parent has committed, aided, or attempted the murder or voluntary manslaughter of a sibling of the child;
- The parent has committed a felony assault resulting in serious bodily injury to the child or a sibling of the child.

Most TPR proceedings arising from child abuse and neglect are initiated by CPS, but in some States, the GAL also can petition on the child's behalf for TPR. ASFA requires that if anyone other than CPS files for TPR, CPS must join in the action.[16]

Ending the Legal Rights and Responsibilities of Parents

Biological parents whose parental rights are terminated as a result of child maltreatment have no right to have contact with the child, knowledge of the child's whereabouts, pictures, or information regarding the child. In addition to losing legal rights to the child, parents whose rights have been terminated generally have no further responsibilities to the child, except to pay child support that is past due. Because of the seriousness and finality of the consequences, TPR has been called the "death penalty" of family law.

There are exceptions. Children who are old enough to remember and to know how to contact their parents may choose to do so. Some children are never adopted and remain in foster care; others are returned to foster care because of a disrupted adoption or because they were abused or neglected by an adoptive or other surrogate parent. In these situations, the original parents may be the best placement option if their circumstances have improved to the point that they pose less risk of harm to the children and if the children are older and better able to protect themselves.

Termination of Parental Rights Petitions and Service

Drafted by the CPS attorney, TPR petitions will allege facts that, if proven, would satisfy the grounds for termination in State law. In many States, TPR is a separate action from the child maltreatment case and sometimes must be filed in a different court. When it is a separate action, the complaint or petition and summons should be served on each of the parents.

Every effort should be made to locate both parents and to serve them personally. The burden of locating parents likely will fall on the CPS caseworker, which can be a difficult and time-consuming process, particularly if one or both parents has disappeared while the child maltreatment proceeding was pending or if one of the parents was never located and served at the start of that case.

Each State has a process for providing notice to the parents, or "constructive service," if a parent cannot be located after diligent efforts. Constructive service can be posting a notice in a legal newspaper or in the courthouse. Although it almost never results in actual notice, it takes time and may involve some expense. One option is to access the Federal Parent Locator Service (FPLS) of the local Federal Child Support Office.[17] (For more information on FPLS, see Chapter 6, *Domestic Relations Cases and Other Court Proceedings*.) Other sources that may yield results are State Department of Motor Vehicles records, State and local prison system records, phone directories, and various online search engines. Agencies are encouraged to develop a routine practice for completing this process, including using form affidavits to document their efforts.

Failure to make legally sufficient service can become grounds for dismissal of the termination petition or for reversal on appeal and consequently can disrupt the child's placement. In States where TPR is a dispositional alternative, service is a less complicated process, provided that each parent was served with the petition in the underlying child maltreatment action. It may be sufficient to mail the notice to the respondent's last known address. Notice of the proceeding and its time and location still should be served, but the process is less formal and technical.

Termination of Parental Rights Trials

TPR cases rely heavily on what happened in the underlying child abuse and neglect cases. In some States, some of the findings of the court in child abuse or neglect cases may be admissible as evidence to prove aspects of the termination case.[18] Most importantly, a trial will focus on what the parents did or did not do since CPS became involved and on what CPS did to support the parents' efforts to regain custody of the child. There are appellate laws in almost every State related to TPR cases, and reversals and remands for retrial frequently are based on perceived CPS shortcomings. Caseworkers who anticipate testifying in TPR trials need to be thoroughly familiar with the history of the case, including the details of everything CPS offered to do or did for the parents and how the parents responded.

TPR cases take longer than other child maltreatment proceedings, but predicting how long is largely guesswork. Scheduling and concluding them, therefore, is a chronic problem in most courts. Frequently, they are tried piecemeal for a few hours or half days at a time. Each rescheduling of successive sessions of the trial requires finding a date and time that is satisfactory for all essential participants. Such an approach often delays conclusion of the case and permanency for the child for months. Some courts have addressed this problem by establishing "long cause" calendars for cases that do not fi t into the normal, relatively short scheduling blocks of the juvenile court. Others courts may set aside large blocks of time on future calendars in anticipation of having protracted TPR trials. CPS can urge courts to adopt these or other scheduling practices that permit termination cases to be tried from beginning to end on consecutive days.

Mediation

Mediation also can be an effective alternative to formal termination proceedings. In courts where it is an option, it often results in voluntary relinquishment of the child by the parents. Rather than focusing on parents' failures or inadequacies, mediation focuses on the child's needs and how they can best be met, and it offers parents an opportunity to make a self-sacrificing choice to give their child a safe and stable future. Most often, it is successful in States that allow "open adoptions" or "adoptions with contact" or that otherwise permits parents to receive information about their child, including letters and photographs, or even limited personal contact. Such agreements may not be enforceable depending on State law, but even where they are not, parents may choose to trust the good will of prospective adoptive parents, particularly if their identities are known, and commit to honoring a continuing contact agreement.

Burden of Proof and Best Interest Issues

TPR usually involves two issues. First, CPS must prove by "clear and convincing evidence" that one or more of the grounds for termination exist.[19] Note that this is a higher burden of proof than is required in many States to prove child abuse and neglect. The "clear and convincing evidence" is also a higher burden of proof for TPR than what existed prior to the *Santosky v. Kramer* decision upholding due process under the 14th Amendment. In this case, the Supreme Court found that a "fair preponderance of evidence" is not sufficient to terminate parental rights, and that "before a State may sever completely and irrevocably the rights of parents in their natural child, due process requires that the State support its allegations by at least clear and convincing evidence."[20]

If the court finds that CPS has met the burden of proof with respect to at least one ground for termination, it will proceed to the second issue— whether termination is in the best interest of the child. CPS can enhance the prospects for a favorable decision by preparing a report weighing the pros and cons of termination from the child's point of view and by being prepared to testify regarding the best interest issue. The prospect of a safe, stable, and permanent home is a strong selling point when contrasted with the likelihood that the child cannot return home safely within any reasonable period of time.

Some courts insist on a showing of adoptability before termination will be ordered, although the basic goal and premise of ASFA is that all children are adoptable. It obviously is more difficult to find adoptive homes for some children than for others, but if children are not "cleared for adoption," meaning that their parents' rights have not been terminated, adoption agencies may not actively pursue adoptive placements. If agencies cannot place them, they will not be adopted.

ADOPTIONS

Children placed for adoption by CPS are entitled to a timely placement with an adoptive family. When parents' rights have been terminated, their child's involvement with juvenile court does not end at the TPR hearing. CPS caseworkers should continue to participate in post-hearing activities to ensure that CPS is complying with ASFA requirements, incorporating Federal adoption legislation into practice, and accessing a variety of adoption subsidies and post-adoption services for eligible children.

Post-Termination Reviews

Many post-termination reviews, or post-permanency hearings, will focus on whether CPS has made reasonable efforts to recruit an adoptive placement. The reasonable efforts inquiry might question whether the agency has an effective recruitment program for adoptive parents and whether its adoption program is adequately and expertly staff ed, knowledgeable about subsidies and interstate placements, and able to provide appropriate post-adoption services. In cases involving special needs children, CPS may be asked whether it is utilizing the specialized agencies that serve these populations. Caseworkers will want to be prepared to respond to such inquiries.

The Multi-Ethnic Placement Act

Another issue that may arise at hearings to review efforts to place children available for adoption is whether the agency is complying with the Multi-Ethnic Placement Act (MEPA) of 1994, as amended by the Inter-Ethnic

Adoption Provisions of 1996, laws that prohibit discrimination in foster care and adoption. These acts provide that States may not "...deny to any person the opportunity to become an adoptive or foster parent on the basis of the race, color, or national origin of the person or of the child involved; or. ..delay or deny the placement of a child for adoption or into foster care on the basis of the race, color or national origin of the adoptive or foster parent or the child involved...." [21]

MEPA primarily addresses considerations in finding out-of-home placements. During court proceedings regarding placements, the judge may ask about compliance with this and other pertinent laws, particularly if there is an aggrieved party contesting the placement. Therefore, caseworkers must be prepared to document compliance so it can be submitted in the court documents. MEPA also requires that special efforts be made to recruit minority foster and adoptive homes.

The Interstate Compact on Adoption and Medical Assistance

The Interstate Compact on Adoption and Medical Assistance (ICAMA) addresses medical and other post-adoption services, as well as payment for those services, for the ongoing needs of children who are adopted across State lines. Not all States are signatories to ICAMA. T ose that are have a designated ICAMA administrator who can be an invaluable source of assistance to caseworkers in ensuring post-adoption services for children placed across State lines.

ICAMA is important since ASFA requires State child welfare plans to:

- Specify that the State will not deny or delay the placement of a child for adoption when an approved family is available outside of the court jurisdiction that has the responsibility for handling the case of the child;
- Contain assurances that the State will develop plans for the effective use of cross-jurisdictional resources to facilitate timely adoptive or permanent placements for waiting children.[22]

Interstate placements also need to comply with the Interstate Compact on the Placement of Children. (See Chapter 3, *The Interplay Between Child Maltreatment Legislation and Caseworker Practice*, for more information.)

Again, the caseworker needs to provide full documentation for court records that ICAMA was adhered to before the adoption or placement is legalized; otherwise, the home State may not pay for this assistance.

Adoption Assistance Subsidies

Parents adopting children who are "IV-E eligible" are entitled to receive a subsidy. According to amendments to the Social Security Act, a child is IV-E eligible if the family from which the child was removed was eligible for Aid to Families with Dependent Children, as the program existed on July 16, 1996, and the child is classified as having "special needs." (See below for more information about special needs. A child classified as having special needs also is IV-E eligible if receiving Supplemental Security Income (42 U.S.C. 673(2)).[23]

Special needs are defined differently by each State and may include:

- A sibling group of two or more;
- An ethnic background that is non-Caucasian;
- Any child age 6 or older;
- A documented physical, mental, or developmental disability or disorder, or an emotional disturbance or behavior problem;
- An identified or reasonably identifiable risk of developing a physical or developmental disability, mental disability or disorder, emotional disturbance, or behavioral problem that is related to the child's history of abuse or neglect, genetic factors, or other environmental traumas;
- Psychological attachment to the foster caregiver due to placement of at least 1 year, such that placement with another family would not be in the child's best interests.

Caseworkers will need to know and be able to apply the definition of special needs to children in their States. States have discretion to determine the amount of the subsidy, but it cannot be greater than the amount that a family would have received if the child was in foster care. They can pay more if the additional amount can be supported through State or local funding. The State can make subsidy payments to a family until the adopted child is 18, but can extend assistance to age 21 for children who are disabled physically or mentally. All special needs children who are IV-E eligible, and most who are not, also are eligible for Medicaid. States are required to provide the same subsidies for special needs children who are not IV-E eligible as they provide for those who are, except that for children who are not IV-E eligible:

- Eligibility can be limited based on family income;
- All funding must be from State or local sources.

Caseworkers need to be able to inform prospective adoptive parents of the financial assistance and medical insurance to which the child will be entitled. Additionally, the courts often will ask if the caseworkers are aware of all available assistance and whether it has been provided to the adoptive parents or special needs children. Therefore, caseworkers should document all efforts to help adoptive parents secure appropriate financial assistance and insurance.

Post-Adoption Services

Adequate financial and health care support of children is critical to the ultimate success of an adoption. The same is true of post-adoption services, which may include providing information and referrals, parent training, education and support groups, individual and family counseling, respite care, and home- based or residential treatment services. The details of the financial support and other services adoptive parents will receive or have available to them must be put in writing, along with information about what they can do if their circumstances change or other unanticipated issues arise. The court will require documentation to ascertain that, in addition to receiving adoption assistance, provisions have been made for post-adoption services, as well as a follow- up schedule to ensure that the adoptive parents have received such services. This documentation is particularly important in cases where the adoption is disrupted. CPS caseworkers also will want to be prepared to respond to any inquiry from the court as to whether the subsidy and other post-adoption supports are sufficient to ensure reasonably that the adoption will be a permanent placement.

APPEALS

Parents and CPS have the right to appeal some decisions of the juvenile court in child abuse and neglect and TPR cases. At the very least, the right to appeal attaches at the conclusion of any adjudication, disposition, or TPR trial. Some States may allow appeal from other trial court orders or decisions, but generally, only final decisions are appealed or accepted for appellate review.

Appellate courts decide cases based on the written record, or a videotape in some locations, from the trial court. They examine the record and determine whether:

- The trial judge abused his or her discretion in finding the facts;
- The facts support the judge's conclusions of the law;
- The judge correctly applied the law to the facts.

Although the child is the subject of the litigation, the child is not a "party" and, depending on the laws of that State, may not have an independent right to appeal. In States that have intermediate appellate courts, appeals most likely will be addressed to these courts. In other States, the appeal will be made directly to the State Supreme Court.

The appellate process often is extremely slow. Orders, transcripts, and appellate briefs need to be prepared, filed, and selected for submission to the appellate court. Appellate judges should confer, make a tentative decision, and identify one member to write the opinion. Negotiations over the decision can take considerable time in cases where there are significant differences of opinion. It is not uncommon for this process to take more than a year from the time of the trial court's decision until an appellate opinion is published. Meanwhile, the child, parents, and foster or adoptive parents are in limbo. Some State appellate courts have attempted to correct this problem by prioritizing the completion of cases.[24]

End Notes

[1] *Tenenbaum v. Williams,* 193 F.3d 581, 596 (2nd Cir. 1999); *Nicholson v. Williams,* 181 F. Supp. 2d 182 (E.D.N.Y. 2002).

[2] Hardin, M. (1992). *Judicial implementation of permanency planning reform: One court that works.* Washington, DC: American Bar Association, Center on Children and the Law; Hardin, M., Rubin, H. T., & Ratterman-Baker, D. (1995). *A second court that works: Judicial implementation of permanency planning reforms.* Washington, DC: American Bar

Association, Center on Children and the Law; National Council of Juvenile and Family Court Judges. (1995). *Resource guidelines: Improving court practice in child abuse and neglect cases*. Reno, NV: Author.

[3] 42 U.S.C. 671(a)(15) (1999).

[4] National Council of Juvenile and Family Court Judges. (1995).

[5] Chandler, S., & Giovannucci, M. (2004). Family group conferencing: Transforming traditional child welfare policy and practice. *Family Court Review, 42*(2), 216–231.

[6] National Council of Juvenile and Family Court Judges. (1995).

[7] Adoption and Safe Families Act of 1997, Pub. L. No. 105–89, § 101 (1997).

[8] Adoption and Safe Families Act of 1997, Pub. L. No. 105–89, § 107 (1997).

[9] National Council of Juvenile and Family Court Judges. (1995).

[10] Adoption and Safe Families Act of 1997, Pub. L. No. 105–89, § 103 (1997).

[11] Adoption and Safe Families Act of 1997, Pub. L. No. 105–89, § 302 (1997).

[12] Child Welfare Information Gateway. (2003). *Determining the best interests of the child: Summary of state laws* [On-line]. Available: http://www. childwelfare.gov/systemwide/ laws_policies/statutes/ best_interestall.pdf.

[13] Adoption and Safe Families Act of 1997, Pub. L. No. 105–89, § 101 (1997).

[14] Adoption and Safe Families Act of 1997, Pub. L. No. 105–89, § 101 (1997).

[15] FindLaw. (n.d.). *U.S. Supreme Court, Santosky v. Kramer,* 455 U.S. 745 (1982) [On-line]. Available: http://caselaw.lp.findlaw.com/scripts=US& vol=455&invol=745.

[16] Adoption and Safe Families Act of 1997, Pub. L. No. 105–89, § 103 (1997); 42 U.S.C. § 675(5)(3) (1997).

[17] Adoption and Safe Families Act of 1997, Pub. L. No. 105–89, § 105 (1997).

[18] National Council of Juvenile and Family Court Judges. (1995).

[19] Child Welfare Information Gateway. (2004). *Grounds for involuntary termination of parental rights* [On-line]. Available: http://www.childwelfare.gov/ systemwide/laws_policies/ statutes/groundterminall. pdf.

[20] *Santosky v. Kramer*, 455 U.S. 745 (1982).

[21] The Multi-Ethnic Placement Act of 1994, Pub. L. No. 103–382, 42 U.S.C. § 5115a (1994); The Inter- Ethnic Adoption Provisions of 1996, Pub. L. No. 104–188 (1996).

[22] Adoption and Safe Families Act of 1997, Pub. L. No. 105–89, § 202 (1997).

[23] U.S. House of Representatives, Committee on Ways and Means. (2004). *2004 Green Book* [Online]. Available: http://waysandmeans.house.gov/ Documents.asp?section=8 13.

[24] Keith, A. L., & Flango, C. R. (2002). *Iowa Court Rules, Appeals in Termination Cases, Rules 6.5–6.154*. Retrieved July 1, 2003, from LexisNexis database.

In: Working with the Courts in Child Protection ISBN: 978-1-61668-303-0
Editors: Raymond T. Devon

Chapter 5

THE CRIMINAL COURT PROCESS

Conduct that rises to the level of child abuse or neglect may constitute a crime, depending on State law and the circumstances of the case; not all criminal acts, however, are prosecuted. Some prosecutors are less zealous than others, or they may believe that all but the most serious of intra-family offenses are best addressed in the juvenile court. Other reasons to forgo prosecution are that it may interfere with rehabilitating families or be traumatic for the children, particularly if they have to testify. Cases typically prosecuted include sex offenses or those that result in the death of, or serious injury to, a child.

Child protective services (CPS) caseworkers may have information about the family that is critical to the criminal court proceeding. Caseworkers always should determine whether either parent or any potential caretaker in a child abuse and neglect case has a criminal record or pending criminal charges. This information can inform a caseworker's assessment of potential risk to the child and enhance case planning and service coordination activities.

While the criminal court process may vary across jurisdictions include:

- Arrest, bail, and other conditions of release;
- Preliminary hearings;
- Discovery;
- Plea bargaining;
- Trial.

ARREST, BAIL AND OTHER CONDITIONS OF RELEASE

Criminal prosecutions most commonly begin with an arrest. Defendants then are brought before a judicial officer (a judge, magistrate, or commissioner) who informs them of the charges against them and determines the conditions of their release pending trial.

The defendant will be notified of the conditions that must be met to be released from police custody before the trial. Defendants with stable residence and employment histories and no significant prior records often are released on their own recognizance or with a written promise to appear at subsequent court dates. For defendants who seem less reliable, a cash bond may be required. Defendants can post the full amount of the bond in cash or property or secure a bondsman for a percentage of that amount. If the defendant flees, the bondsman is obligated to pay the full amount of the bond. The judge also has the discretion to impose other conditions of release, including the defendant having no contact with the child or other parent or not returning to the residence.

CPS caseworkers can assist with protecting the child and the non-off ending parent by reporting to the prosecutor any violation of a "no contact" or "stay away" condition. In such cases, the caseworker can encourage the prosecutor to ask the criminal court judge to revoke the defendant's bond and return him to jail.

PRELIMINARY HEARINGS

The purpose of a preliminary hearing is to determine whether there is probable cause to believe that the defendant committed the alleged offense and that he should be tried on that charge. If the judge finds no probable cause, the case will be dismissed. If the judge finds probable cause, the case will be transferred to the trial court for resolution.

Witnesses sometimes are called to testify and are cross-examined at preliminary hearings. The CPS caseworker or the child may be among them. As a general rule, CPS caseworkers should discourage having the child testify, except possibly in cases where there is no other way to establish probable cause. Because they may be asked to recount painful memories in a public and contentious environment, children may find testifying in court to be traumatic and uncomfortable. (See Chapter 7, *Going to Court*, for more information on children's testimony.)

In some States, evidence of criminal conduct by the defendant is presented at a preliminary hearing to a grand jury instead of a judge. The grand jury then determines whether the evidence is sufficient to constitute probable cause. If so, the grand jury will issue an indictment that also puts the case before the trial court. Only the prosecutor and State's witnesses, usually the investigating law enforcement officer, appear before the grand jury. It is unlikely that either the CPS caseworker or a child would be asked to testify. Neither the defendant nor the defense attorney has the right to be present at that proceeding.

DISCOVERY

Discovery refers to the process of obtaining information about the charge from the opposing party and, at times, other sources. It is less accessible and less extensively used in criminal cases than in civil actions, including child abuse and neglect proceedings, due to more stringent legal requirements. Defendants in some States, however, may be entitled to access CPS records, particularly if they contain information or evidence that may be helpful to their defense. The identity of reporters of child maltreatment, however, still may be withheld.

PLEA BARGAINING

Plea bargaining is to the criminal process what settlements are to the juvenile court process. These negotiated resolutions conclude the majority of both types of cases. Without them, courts could not reach all the cases to be tried on a timely basis.

Plea bargaining, which results in avoiding trial, has the added benefit in child abuse and neglect cases of eliminating the need for the child to testify and of speeding the resolution of the case, both of which relieve the child's anxiety. Nevertheless, there also may be negative consequences to a plea bargain. Depending on the sentence, the child victim may feel betrayed, disbelieved, or unsafe. In addition, the public may perceive that child maltreatment is not taken as seriously as other crimes.

TRIAL

If no plea bargain is reached, the case goes to trial. In criminal trials, the rules of evidence are applied strictly, and the prosecutor has a greater burden of proof. In order to convict, the jurors must unanimously find "beyond a reasonable doubt" that the defendant committed the alleged offense. This is a much higher burden of proof than the "clear and convincing evidence" standard in termination of parental rights trials in some States' child abuse and neglect actions. It is higher still than the "preponderance or greater weight of the evidence" standard in civil cases generally and in child abuse and neglect cases in some States.

CPS caseworkers should know if any criminal charges were filed stemming from the facts and circumstances related to their child abuse and neglect cases. The caseworker will want to establish and to maintain contact with the prosecutor responsible for those charges to know when events in the case are scheduled, whether the child maybe called as a witness, or the terms of any plea offer. The prosecutor needs to be informed of the status of the child abuse and neglect case, the case plan, and how the prosecution can benefit from that plan. To ensure that provisions important to the child and the case plan are considered, the caseworker should ask to participate in any bond hearing or plea negotiations and in the sentencing process. However, the criminal court judge may operate independently of the juvenile court and may give little or no weight to what the caseworker requests.

The criminal court case may be concluded well after the disposition hearing in the child abuse and neglect case, and its outcome can be inconsistent with the case plan and the best resolution of the child abuse and neglect case. The opposite also can be true, and the criminal sentence can augment and enhance the case plan and the prospects for a positive outcome. In communities where the same prosecutor represents the public interest in both criminal and child abuse and neglect cases, there is greater likelihood of a coordinated approach to resolving both matters. In communities where different offices are responsible for the two types of cases, the CPS caseworker should do as much as possible to ensure that the outcome in criminal court complements and supports the case plan in the juvenile case.

The desired court outcomes might vary from case to case. For example, in a case where the mother's boyfriend has been abusive to her and the child, the caseworker may advocate that he be incarcerated for the maximum period possible. On the other hand, if he is an important figure in the child's life, has been participating successfully in a batterers' intervention program, is the principal breadwinner for the family, and the plan is reunification of all family members, then a lengthy sentence would be contrary to the case plan. A suspended sentence and probation, with conditions consistent with the case plan, could enhance prospects for the plan's success. This scenario would not impose a fine or other financial burdens that would interfere with the defendant's ability to support the family.

Frequently, a parent or other caretaker in a child abuse and neglect case will be on probation for some unrelated criminal offense (e.g., a drug charge) and be required as a condition of probation to complete a drug treatment program successfully. The threat of incarceration can be a powerful motivator for overcoming a substance abuse habit or for changing other behaviors. The caseworker will want to establish and to maintain contact with the probation officer to stay abreast of the defendant's compliance with the conditions of probation. This level of coordination of the two processes is uncommon, but positive results can be realized when the CPS caseworker establishes a good working relationship with the probation officer.

Communicating with the prosecutor and the probation officer in criminal cases involving the parents or other caretakers of children who have been maltreated is an important role for CPS caseworkers and other involved service providers. Sharing information and coordinating agency efforts with what happens in criminal court to achieve a safe, permanent home for children can produce beneficial results in a CPS case.

In: Working with the Courts in Child Protection ISBN: 978-1-61668-303-0
Editors: Raymond T. Devon

Chapter 6

DOMESTIC RELATIONS CASES AND OTHER COURT PROCEEDINGS

Families involved with child protective services (CPS) often face multiple problems and complex challenges, some of which require court involvement. Matters involving child maltreatment or juvenile delinquency typically are resolved in juvenile court. Other issues affecting families frequently are addressed in other court venues. CPS caseworkers who work with families struggling with divorce, domestic violence, and mental health problems may fi nd these families involved in other court processes. As well as understanding the juvenile court process, CPS caseworkers also should be familiar with other court hearings that affect families and case practice.

This chapter provides an overview of three types of court hearings that may involve CPS families— custody and divorce, domestic violence, and mental health hearings. The chapter also discusses suits against CPS caseworkers and agencies and Federal class actions against agencies.

CUSTODY AND DIVORCE HEARINGS

Allegations of child abuse or neglect may arise in custody and divorce cases, which result from the separation of married partners or the estrangement of unmarried parents. These also are known in some places as matrimonial or domestic relations cases.

Actions between spouses may include claims for the division of marital property, spousal support and, when the couple has minor children, custody, visitation, and child support. Actions between unmarried parents often are referred to as paternity cases and involve the issues of paternity, custody, and child support.

CPS Involvement in Custody Cases

Domestic relations, paternity, and domestic violence cases are civil actions, and unlike child abuse and neglect cases, they take place between private individuals. CPS may become involved, however, if allegations of child abuse or neglect are made against a parent or someone living in the parent's home. In these circumstances, CPS has the challenge of determining whether to substantiate a complaint made in the context of what often is an acrimonious battle between parents over their child. There is a temptation, therefore, to discount these complaints. CPS must be careful, however, to conduct a thorough investigation that considers the context and objectively evaluates other facts. Retaining a neutral, well- trained, experienced, and widely respected custody evaluator may be useful.[1]

If abuse or neglect is substantiated, deciding whether to try the case in the domestic relations or the juvenile court can be an issue. CPS should not file a petition alleging child abuse or neglect if the non abusive parent is committed to protecting the child and if the court adopts an access and visitation plan that will keep the child safe. However, if CPS doubts that the parent or the court will protect the child from harm, it may choose to file a petition in juvenile court. In most States, the jurisdiction of the juvenile court to determine whether a child is abused or neglected will take precedence over a custody determination by the domestic relations court. Custody and visitation issues can be relegated to domestic relations or juvenile court upon showing that circumstances have changed substantially in ways that affect the child.

Motions to change custody or visitation frequently include allegations of child abuse as a basis for the motion. CPS needs to address these allegations as if they were new cases. For example, when a father is charged with a sex offense against his child and there is a pending custody proceeding, the domestic relations court, the criminal court, or both usually will order either no visitation or supervised visitation. If the father is acquitted or the charge is dismissed in criminal court, he may come to the domestic relations court requesting unsupervised visitation on that basis. The court's decision about custody and visitation, however, is independent of the criminal process. The domestic relations court judge must hear evidence and decide whether the child was sexually abused by the father and, if so, what to do about visitation.

Caseworkers should keep in mind that the burden of proof in criminal cases is "beyond a reasonable doubt," a much higher standard than the "preponderance of or greater weight of the evidence" standard in custody cases. Criminal charges are dismissed for a variety of reasons including the age of the child, the trauma to the child testifying, or insufficient credible evidence to prove the charge. A dismissal or an acquittal on those charges is not necessarily a determination that the defendant was innocent of the charge.

In this scenario, if the domestic relations court allows visitation that, in the judgment of CPS, will result in abuse of the child, CPS can file a child abuse and neglect petition in juvenile court, which also would hear the evidence and make an independent decision as to whether the father had sexually abused the child. If it is determined that he did, the juvenile court could order either more restricted visitation or no visitation.

Family Courts

The complex relationships among different courts and potentially conflicting decisions can cause confusion among practitioners and family members. These issues are some of the driving force behind the rising popularity and implementation of family courts. (See Chapter 2, *The Court System and Child Protection*, for a description of family courts.) In a model family court, the same judge would hear the domestic relations, the domestic violence, and the child abuse and neglect cases. Family courts can offer multiple benefits:

- Minimizing the potential for conflicting orders and outcomes;
- Improving coordination among the court interventions;
- Reducing the number of court appearances;
- Enhancing the judge's familiarity with the issues and the parties;
- Bringing about a more successful end result.

While most courts are not organized, equipped, or legally able to achieve the "one family-one judge model," many are moving as far as possible in that direction. For example, some courts are making beneficial services, such as those listed below, more readily available and are committed to resolving family conflicts with minimal negative impact on the children.

Case Management and Services

Domestic relations courts can provide essential case management and services to families appearing before them. While not the case in every State, well-resourced domestic relations courts use case managers to:

- Ensure that discovery, motions, requests for temporary relief (e.g., spousal or child support), or other pretrial issues are addressed and resolved on schedule;
- Monitor the completion of mandatory actions, such as parent education or mediation;
- Keep the case on track for a timely, final resolution;
- Identify and facilitate the delivery of services to children and parties (whether they are available through the court or elsewhere).

The following are services offered by some domestic relations courts:

- **Mediation**—a process focusing on how parents will share responsibility for their children in the future. Facilitated by a trained mediator, mediation can be effective in resolving custody disputes without a trial.
- **Custody evaluations**—evaluative services for parents and children that can be useful to the court in making custody and visitation determinations. These services sometimes are publicly funded and other times available only from private providers at the expense of the litigants.
- **Guardians ad Litem (GAL)**—lawyers appointed by some courts for the children in custody and visitation cases, particularly if there are allegations of maltreatment or domestic violence, or if the conflict between the parents is unusually high. These GALs typically are not associated with the GAL or CASA Program in the juvenile court.
- **Parent education programs**—courses for separating parents that can help them understand how their children may be affected by the separation and what they can do to minimize adverse effects.

- **Supervised visitation and exchange services**— programs that off er safe, comfortable settings and trained professionals to protect a child's safety during parental visits. In some programs, the supervisor will coach a parent on how to engage the child or on how to interact more appropriately with the child or with the other parent. They often will involve the use of intermediaries to transfer the child between the parents.
- **Parenting coordination**—a relatively new service, typically used in high-conflict cases, that employs a mental health professional to support and to assist parents in implementing a parenting agreement or court order. A parenting coordinator can help parents settle their differences and can enable them to avoid the time, emotional trauma, and expense of returning repeatedly to court.[2]

The above services also may be beneficial in some child abuse and neglect cases. CPS caseworkers will want to know how to access them, particularly when parents or family members are vying for custody or visitation of a child in a maltreatment case.

Child Support

Many children in child abuse and neglect proceedings have unmet economic needs. Most live with one or neither of their biological parents, and of those, many do not receive any child support. CPS should, therefore, place a priority on locating biological parents, establishing paternity (if necessary), and pursuing child support and medical insurance from an absent parent. In fact, reasonable efforts requirements mandate that CPS do so.

Establishment of paternity and establishment and enforcement of child support and medical insurance obligations for foster children are by law the responsibility of Child Support Enforcement (CSE).[3] Every community has access to a CSE office, and in many places, they are co-located with, and operated by, the same agency as CPS. Caseworkers who are attempting to keep a family together need to help the family access CSE services.

Some courts establish paternity during child abuse and neglect proceedings, often at the initial hearing or the adjudication, provided the putative father is willing to consent to the entry of a judgment of paternity. When a putative father denies paternity or is not willing to acknowledge it formally, the case must be referred immediately to CSE. Genetic testing will be done, and in almost all cases, the results of that testing will be conclusive. CSE can initiate paternity establishment for putative fathers living in other States when requested to do so by CPS.

FEDERAL PARENT LOCATOR SERVICE

The Federal Parent Locator Service (FPLS) is an automated information system maintained by the Federal Office of Child Support Enforcement (OCSE). FPLS is a vast database that includes Social Security numbers, names of employers, and information on income and personal assets. It is used by CSE to locate persons who may be the father of a child or a parent who has a child support obligation. The Adoption and Safe Families Act (P.L. 105–89) requires that the resources of FPLS also be available to CPS for locating parents in its cases.[4] FPLS is an invaluable resource for caseworkers who need to fi nd and serve a putative father or absent parent.

Some courts have developed working agreements or protocols with CSE and CPS to facilitate the establishment of paternity, as well as the establishment and enforcement of support obligations, and to speed access to FPLS. These strategies may include locating OCSE staff and computers near the juvenile court to serve the parent and to help identify the paternity and child support needs of the children and families in that court. Judges have to ensure that all has been done to locate the missing parent, not only for the enforcement of child support, but also for placement options or for termination of parental rights. Therefore, the courts may require documentation from the caseworker regarding utilization of this service.

Support payments made by the parents reduce CPS's (or a relative's) costs for providing for the child. The amount of child support owed by an absent parent is determined in every State by the application of a child support guideline or formula. The guidelines are based on the assumption that one parent pays support to the other. Additionally, parents whose children were already receiving child support and have been placed in foster care often have difficulty regaining custody for financial reasons. They may need housing, furnishings, security and utility deposits, or other services. The amount of their child support payments should not preclude them from having the funds necessary to achieve reunification. In these circumstances, caseworkers may want to request that a reduction of the child support payments be considered. For the same reason, consideration must be given to suspending repayment of past public assistance or arrearages.

DOMESTIC VIOLENCE HEARINGS

While children should not be removed unnecessarily, neither should they be left in environments that jeopardize their safety. This has been a particularly problematic issue in cases where children are exposed to domestic violence. As CPS caseworkers become increasingly aware of the high co-occurrence of domestic violence and child maltreatment and of the potential emotional impact of exposure to domestic violence on children, more communities are filing child maltreatment petitions in such cases and requesting removal of the children.[5] Research indicates that children exposed to domestic abuse are more likely to experience physical abuse or neglect than children living in nonviolent homes.[6] Studies estimate that there are adult and child victims in 30 to 60 percent of families experiencing domestic violence, and for adult victims who experience severe forms of domestic abuse, their children are in danger of suffering serious physical harm.[7]

CPS caseworkers should recognize that "[c]hildhood exposure to adult domestic violence should not automatically be defined as maltreatment...." Instead, "[w]hat's needed... are empirical and practice-based criteria for deciding whether or not a child is at a heightened risk of harm" before placing an undue burden on the victim by removing the child.[8] Once established, these criteria must be developed into effective screening and assessment instruments for use in the field. In addition, there is a dire need to develop greater expertise within child protection agencies about domestic violence, to collaborate with domestic violence programs, and to provide alternative forms of voluntary, community- based services for exposed children and their families, including specialized parenting and intervention programs for the perpetrator.[9]

The process for filing actions for protection against domestic violence is designed to accommodate persons who do not have an attorney. Complaint forms are available, no filing fee is required, and most jurisdictions afford relatively prompt access to a judicial officer at any hour of the day or night. Litigants often request, and are able to obtain immediately, an *ex parte* order granting eviction of the alleged abusers from the parties' residence or other protective relief. Additionally, in best case scenarios, the time from filing to final hearing and conclusion of the case can be brief, ranging from a few days to a few weeks at most. For these reasons, claims for protection against domestic violence usually are filed as separate actions. Exhibit 6-1 provides more information about protection orders.

EXHIBIT 6-1. DOMESTIC VIOLENCE PROTECTIVE ORDERS

Claims for protection against domestic violence sometimes are brought in conjunction with a domestic relations case, but more often they are filed separately. These are variously known as protective orders, restraining orders, or orders of protection. These orders are available in every State and may require that the abusive partner:

- Be evicted from the parties' residence, not return there, or not go to where the victim works;
- Refrain from abusing the victim;
- Have no contact with the victim;
- Participate in substance abuse treatment or a batterers' intervention program;
- Pay support.

The order also may include protection for the children and may award custody of the children and child support. Not all of these remedies are available in every State, but statutes usually authorize the court to impose any additional terms or conditions it deems necessary for the victim's protection. In most States, orders granting relief in domestic violence cases are limited in duration from 1 to 5 years.

Federal law also makes possession of a firearm illegal for anyone who is subject to an active protective order that meets specified criteria. Some States and judges go further and order defendants against whom a protective order is issued to surrender all weapons to a law enforcement agency and to not purchase or possess any firearm as long as the order remains in effect. Possessing a firearm also is illegal for any individual who has ever been convicted of certain domestic violence crimes.[10]

Domestic violence protection or restraining orders should be logged immediately into a State's central registry as well as the National Crime Information Center Protection Order File, which can be accessed by any law enforcement officer. These orders are enforceable across State lines.[11] Violation of the order is a separate criminal offense in most States and will result in immediate arrest of defendants who are caught violating it. If the defendants are not caught, but there is probable cause to believe they violated an order, a warrant for their arrests can be issued. Alternatively, violations can subject the offenders to being found in contempt of court and punished by fines or incarceration.

CPS caseworkers with cases in which family violence is a significant problem will want to consider the efficacy of a protection order. This may involve encouraging the victim to take the actions necessary to obtain the order, or in some jurisdictions, CPS may request a protective order in the child maltreatment case. A victim should not be compelled, however, to choose between obtaining or abiding by an order and having the child removed by CPS. It is important to respect the victim's opinion of what would enhance the children's safety or would place them at greater risk. Protection orders can contribute to the safety of adult and child victims of domestic violence, but they do not ensure safety. Those orders often are violated, sometimes resulting in serious injury or even the death of the parent or children. Domestic violence victims' advocates can provide CPS caseworkers with recommendations to engage adult victims in the protection and safety of themselves and their children.

Mental Health Hearings

Some children in foster care are committed involuntarily or are admitted voluntarily to mental health treatment facilities. The CPS caseworker should work with a supervisor and a mental health professional in deciding whether to pursue such a placement and likely will be the person to accompany and to admit the child to the facility. The caseworker also will need to attend the hearing and present CPS's position regarding the child's need for continued treatment. It is unlikely that a CPS lawyer will be present although there may be a prosecutor or a lawyer for the facility. The caseworker will want to communicate with facility staff to learn the child's diagnosis and recommendations for treatment and immediately begin work with staff on a discharge plan that will meet the child's needs. Every effort must be made to avoid extending confinement in the facility because of a lack of appropriate alternative placement.

Some State laws require court approval for the voluntary admission of minors to mental health treatment facilities or for the involuntary commitment of minors or adults. Whether the law applies to a particular placement usually depends on whether it is a locked facility, such as a psychiatric hospital or residential treatment program. Voluntary admissions to mental health treatment facilities are made by a parent, guardian, or CPS for a child. The court must determine whether the child is mentally ill and in need of further treatment. Some States also require that a child not be placed in such facilities if better alternatives are available. Many children object to being admitted, and, from their perspective, the admission is involuntary. While caseworkers need to respect the child's feelings and concerns, they also need to explain the reason for admittance, such as the child being a danger to herself (e.g., suicidal tendencies) or to others. Otherwise, the caseworker should continue to find the least restrictive facility that meets the child's mental health needs. Additionally, the court must decide whether the child is mentally ill or poses a danger.

Statutes governing voluntary admissions and involuntary commitments are intended to protect the liberty interests of patients. They help ensure that the decision to deprive them of their freedom is reviewed independently and objectively and that they will not be held against their will unless a court finds that there is a legally sufficient basis for doing so.

In some States, involuntary commitment and voluntary admissions are the only vehicles for forcibly placing a child in a mental health treatment facility. In others, juvenile court judges can order that children be admitted to such facilities as the disposition for a delinquent or status offense.

Confidentiality of Court Records

The Child Abuse Prevention and Treatment Act (CAPTA) of 1974 required that records of child abuse complaints and investigations be confidential and that court proceedings be closed to the public. CAPTA was reauthorized and amended by Congress, most recently as part of the Keeping Children and Families Safe Act of 2003 (P.L. 108–36). This amendment to CAPTA changed the confidentiality requirements so States now must share confidential information with any Federal, State, or local government entity or agency with a legal responsibility to protect children. In addition, States now can conduct court proceedings at which child abuse and neglect determinations are being made more open without jeopardizing eligibility for CAPTA funds.[12]

SUITS AGAINST CHILD PROTECTIVE SERVICES CASEWORKERS AND AGENCIES

If CPS negligently fails to investigate or to intervene to protect a child when there is reason to believe the child is abused or neglected, and the child is harmed as a result, the child may be able to sue for damages through a GAL or a "next friend," the legal term for an adult who files suit on the child's behalf. A suit also can be filed for maltreatment that occurs in out-of-home care through CPS negligence or willful misconduct. An example is the physical or sexual abuse of a child by a foster parent.

The defendants in suits for damages are likely to be the CPS caseworker, the caseworker's supervisor, the agency director, and the county or State. It is difficult to generalize about the liability of caseworkers because the law on liability is defined largely by appellate decisions and is State-specific. CPS caseworkers will want to know:

- What the law regarding their liability is in the State where they work;
- Whether they have any immunity from liability and, if so, the extent of that immunity;
- Whether CPS insures them for liability and the extent of that protection;
- Whether CPS or any insurance carrier will provide legal representation for a caseworker who is sued.

Caseworkers should request this information from their agency which is frequently named as co-respondent in a suit. The National Center for Field Consultation can provide guidance on coping with child welfare litigation.

CLASS ACTIONS AGAINST AGENCIES

Under some circumstances, a group of individuals who are similarly situated may bring a class action against CPS for violations of Federal law or of the U.S. Constitution. These actions usually address inadequacies in agency services, staffing, or practices. Although individual claims for monetary damages may accompany the claim for class relief, the remedy usually sought is a declaratory judgment or an injunction. A declaratory judgment is a statement by the court about what the law requires of CPS. An injunction is a directive or order requiring CPS to take certain actions or forbidding it from engaging in specified actions.

EXAMPLE OF CLASS ACTION LAWSUIT

One notable example of a class action lawsuit is *Nicholson v. Williams* in New York City. Unlike most other class action suits, it went to trial, and the result was an injunction against the city's Administration for Children Services (ACS). The injunction prohibited ACS from removing "...a child from the custody of the mother without a court order solely because the mother is a victim of domestic violence except in cases where the child is in such imminent danger to life or health that he or she must be removed and there is not reasonably sufficient time to obtain a court order." The injunction also required that petitions not be filed against a mother solely because she "engaged" in domestic violence in the presence of the children or refused to accept services unless the petition alleges with specificity how the child has been harmed. Due to the lawsuit, petitions are required to describe specifically any acts of domestic violence alleged and any harm suff ered by the child as a result of such acts. Additionally, ACS was required to develop new materials and training regarding cases in which domestic violence is an issue, to employ domestic violence specialists, and to conduct a safety conference within 72 hours of the removal of any child from a mother who is a victim of domestic violence and has not otherwise abused or neglected the child.[13]

A number of such lawsuits have been filed in recent years. Most have been settled by agreement of the parties, known as a "consent decree." The relief generally has involved a commitment by CPS to improve practice and service delivery in specified ways. In most cases, the court has appointed a receiver or, more commonly, a review panel to monitor and to assist implementation of the consent decree.

The type of court that hears the case determines who is affected by the decision. State court appellate decisions have the force of law only in the

States in which they are issued. U.S. District Court decisions apply only in the district in which they are issued, and U.S. Court of Appeals (Circuit Courts) decisions apply only in the States of that circuit. U.S. Supreme Court decisions, however, have national reach. Appellate courts of all types often cite decisions from other State or Federal courts to support their own rulings in similar cases.

End Notes

[1] Kuehnle, K. (1996). *Assessing allegations of child sexual abuse.* Sarasota, FL: Professional Resources Press; Gould, J. W., & Martindale, D. A. (in press). *Child maltreatment and child custody.* New York, NY: Guildford Press; Bow, J. N., Quinell, F. A., Saroff , M., & Assemany, A. (2002). Assessment of sexual abuse allegations in child custody cases. *Professional Psychology: Research & Practice, 33*(6), 566–575.

[2] Garrity C. B., & Baris, M. (1994). *Caught in the middle: Protecting the children of high-conflict divorce.* New York, NY: Lexington Press.

[3] The Social Security Act of 1935, 42 U.S.C. Ch. 7, (1996).

[4] National Conference of Commissioners on Uniform State Laws. (2002). *Uniform Child Witness Testimony by Alternative Methods Act* [On-line]. Available: *http://www.i-lawpublishing.net/news/ucwtbama.pdf.*

[5] Baker, L. L., Jaff e, P. G., Berkowitz, S. J., & Berkman, M. (2002). *Children exposed to domestic violence: A handbook for police trainers to increase understanding and improve community responses* [On-line]. Available: http://www.lfcc.on.ca/police-us.PDF.

[6] Appel, A. E., & Holden, G. W. (1998a). The co- occurrence of spouse and physical child abuse: A review and appraisal. *Journal of Family Psychology, 12*(4), 578–599; Edleson, J. L. (1999). The overlap between child maltreatment and woman battering. *Violence Against Women, 5*(2), 134–154.

[7] Appel, A. E., & Holden, G. W. (1998a); Appel, A. E., & Holden, G. W. (1998b). Co-occurring spouse and child abuse: Implications for CPS practice. *APSAC Advisor, 11*(1), 11–14; Barnett, O. W., Miller-Perrin, C. L., & Perrin, R. D. (1997). *Family violence across the lifespan: An introduction.* Thousand Oaks, CA: Sage; Edleson, J. L. (1999); Hughes, H. M., Parkinson, D., & Vargo, M. (1989). Witnessing spouse abuse and experiencing physical abuse: A "double whammy"? *Journal of Family Violence, 4*(2), 197–209.

[8] Edleson, J. L. (2000). *Should childhood exposure to adult domestic violence be defined as child maltreatment under the law?* [On-line]. Available: *http://www. mincava.umn.edu/link/documents/shouldch/* shouldch.shtml.

[9] Edleson, J. L. (2003). Should childhood exposure to adult domestic violence be defined as child maltreatment under the law? *Juvenile and Family Justice Today, 12*(2), 12–14; Baker, L. L., Jaff e, P. G., Berkowitz, S. J., & Berkman, M. (2002); Goodmark, L. (2002). Assessing and treating child victims of domestic violence. *Child Law Practice, 21*(10), 149– 153.

[10] Gun Control Act of 1968, Pub. L. No. 90–618 (1968); 18 U.S.C. § 921 et seq. (2003); Mitchell, D., & Carbon, S. B. (2002). Firearms and domestic violence: A primer for judges. *Journal of the American Judges Association, 39*(2), 32–43.

[11] The Violence Against Women Act of 1994, 18 U.S.C. § 2265 (1994).

[12] Keeping Children and Families Safe Act of 2003, Pub. L. No. 108–36, Title I, Section 114(b) (2003).

[13] *In re Nicholson, et al.* 181 F. Supp. 2d 182, 188 (2002).

In: Working with the Courts in Child Protection ISBN: 978-1-61668-303-0
Editors: Raymond T. Devon

Chapter 7

GOING TO COURT

Most child protective services (CPS) caseworkers are prepared to interview family members, to conduct home visits, to document cases, and to work with other social service providers. However, there is one component of casework practice that leaves some caseworkers anxious and ill-equipped—preparing for and conducting themselves in court.

Simply knowing the different types of court hearings and mastering legal terminology do not demonstrate a caseworker's competence in juvenile court. Skillful courtroom presentation, well-documented court reports, and a collaborative style also are necessary to maximize constructive family, agency, and court outcomes. This chapter presents practical guidelines to help CPS caseworkers prepare themselves for going to court, to help them work with children who also may be called to testify, and to improve their working relationships with the judges.

THE RULES OF EVIDENCE

The rules of evidence determine what information can be introduced in court and for what purposes. They are intended to ensure that the court's decisions are based on reliable information.

Types of Evidence

Evidence takes different forms, specifically:

- **Direct ev**of an eyewitness;
- **Demonstrative evidence** includes items such as documents, photographs, or x-rays;
- **Circumstantial evidence** is indirect evidence from which an inference can be drawn, such as a child with an oddly shaped bruise on her back.

For example, a CPS caseworker's record might contain the following types of evidence:

- The log kept by a teacher of the days the child came to school with noticeable bruises;
- Documentation that a neighbor heard the child's screams;
- The record of the physician who examined the child reporting that she had multiple bruises of different ages and severity on her back and buttocks;
- Photographs of the bruises taken by police;
- Documentation that the child told the CPS caseworker that she lives alone with her mother and that her mother hits her with a belt;
- The belt.

In court, the child's testimony would be direct evidence. The teacher's log, the photographs, and the belt would be demonstrative evidence. Living alone with her mother, coupled with the screams and the bruises, would be circumstantial evidence identifying the mother as the abuser.

All evidence must be both material and relevant to be admitted. To be material, evidence must have a logical connection to an issue in the case. To be relevant, evidence must increase the likelihood that a particular fact is true.

The more caseworkers know about the rules of evidence, the better they can prepare for a case. The burden of proof for the particular stage of the proceeding or type of case determines how much evidence is enough. The judge or jury will decide whether the credible evidence presented satisfies the burden of proof. (See Chapter 4, *The Juvenile Court Process*, for a discussion on adjudication and the burden of proof.)

The Hearsay Rule and Exceptions

The hearsay rule excludes evidence that is unreliable. Hearsay is defined as an out-of-court statement made by someone other than the witness, which is offered for the truth of that statement. For example, the hearsay rule would prevent a caseworker from testifying that a neighbor told the caseworker that she saw the mother hit the child with a belt. For that information to be admitted, the neighbor would have to testify in court. The rule, however, does not exclude out-of-court statements that are not offered for the truth of what was said. For example, a statement by the neighbor that she heard the mother yell, "I'm going to kill you," just before the child's screams would be admitted not for the truth of the statement but to show that the mother said it. The neighbor would not be testifying as to whether the mother actually attempted to kill or to abuse the child, only that she made the statement.

There are numerous exceptions to the hearsay rule that admit evidence that otherwise would be hearsay. These exceptions are based on the existence of other indications that the statements are reliable. Exceptions that are particularly relevant to child abuse and neglect cases include:

- **Admissions**. The mother said to the CPS caseworker, "I know I hit her too hard, but I will not do it again." The caseworker would be allowed to testify to what the mother said, even though it is an out-of-court statement offered for its truth, because it was also the admission of a party. Such an admission is thought to be reliable because it was against the mother's interest to make it.
- **Excited utterances**. An out-of-court statement that is made spontaneously under extreme emotional excitement also may be admissible as an exception to the hearsay rule. An excited utterance is viewed as trustworthy because the speaker's excitement at the time it was made is thought to prevent him or her from refl ecting long enough to fabricate the statement. The length of time between the event and the statement is a critical factor in determining the admissibility of such statements.

- **Regularly kept records**. Records are hearsay because they contain second-hand information, but their contents will be considered reliable and, therefore, admissible when they are kept regularly, systematically, and routinely. The regularity of the record-keeping process by persons with a duty to supply accurate data ensures trustworthiness. The foundation for the admission of records is established by the testimony of the person who made the record or the custodian of the records. This exception may be applied to medical records, police reports, school records, and CPS files. Caseworkers must be careful to record accurately the statements of others and their own observations. The record must be as factual as possible.

There are other exceptions to the hearsay rule, but they are used less commonly in child maltreatment cases.

EXPERT TESTIMONY

Expert testimony is opinion testimony about a subject that is outside the judge or jury's knowledge or experience. The witness needs to show that she is qualified to testify as an expert on a particular subject. These qualifications may be based on experience; education and training; professional accomplishments, recognition, and memberships; prior testimony as an expert; or familiarity with the relevant professional literature. After each party has the opportunity to question the witness, the judge will decide whether the witness may testify as an expert and on what specific subject. Expert witnesses are common in child maltreatment cases. Examples of expert witnesses include:

- Medical doctors who have expertise in the causes of physical injuries or conditions, such as spiral fractures, Shaken Baby Syndrome, failure to thrive, or Munchausen syndrome by proxy;
- Mental health professionals who can diagnose mental illness or can explain issues of bonding and attachment;
- Domestic violence specialists who have the expertise to explain the debilitating eff cts on a child of witnessing the physical abuse of a parent;
- Specialists in child sexual abuse or substance abuse.

To be admitted into evidence, the expert's opinion needs to be relevant, which means that it needs to increase the likelihood that a particular fact is true or that a particular condition exists. The expert's testimony also needs to have a sound scientific basis. Application of these rules can be complicated. It is the CPS attorney's responsibility to identify the need for expert testimony, to prepare the witness to testify, and to demonstrate in court that the witness is qualified and that the testimony is admissible.[1]

COURT REPORTS

Court reports afford caseworkers some of the best opportunities to communicate information to the court and to influence its decision. If CPS or the court has a standard format for such documents, the caseworker will need to use that. Some formats may be ineffective vehicles, however, for quickly imparting critical information. Poorly organized reports frustrate judges and other participants and are less likely to be infl uential. Caseworkers should consider adding a cover page that summarizes key decisions to be made and the CPS position with respect to each of them, including references by title and page number to any attached documentation. References to documents in the court's file should be noted by the title and date of filing.

Case plans and reasonable efforts reports also are valuable for conveying information to the court. As with the court report, they should be comprehensive, concise, and written as directly and clearly as possible. If the document is an updated version of an earlier one, the new material should be highlighted. The goal is to present the material in a manner that is easily understood. In addition, it should be simple to locate any supporting documentation. Judges will appreciate receiving reports that satisfy these criteria and will be able to understand more clearly CPS positions and the reasons for them.

The content of the court report will depend on the type of hearing for which it is presented and the status of the case. (See Chapter 4, *The Juvenile Court Process*, for further information on the issues to be addressed at various hearings over the course of a child maltreatment case.)

TESTIFYING

Speaking to the court and other participants in a case is another excellent opportunity to communicate information that may affect the court's decision.

Relatively few child maltreatment cases are adjudicated by trial, but when one is tried, the caseworker invariably will be called to testify or to give answers under oath. Caseworkers also may be called to give formal testimony at other stages of the court process, particularly the permanency hearing, and usually at any trial related to the termination of parental rights.

More commonly, caseworkers will have the opportunity to testify informally regarding case plans, the child's well-being, reasonable efforts, visitation, parental performance, and needed services at each hearing in the case. This testimony is not under oath and usually is delivered from the CPS counsel table rather than from the witness stand.

Preparation for Testimony

Before every hearing, the caseworker should review the case and be prepared to answer questions about it. The nature of the hearing will determine the types of questions that may be asked. In order to prepare to testify, the caseworker should:

- Become thoroughly familiar with the facts of the case and with the case file;
- Meet with the CPS attorney to discuss the case and the particulars of the testimony, especially any troublesome aspects;
- Identify key facts or points that the attorney will want to elicit;
- Discuss with the attorney the expected cross- examination questions;
- Outline the history of the case, including important dates and events;
- Summarize the services offered, the response, and the outcomes;
- Prepare to answer questions about reasonable efforts;
- Talk with any previous caseworkers about their involvement with the family.

The caseworker also should prepare a description of his professional experience and qualifi cations.

Guidelines for Testifying

During direct examination, the attorney calls the caseworker to be a witness and asks questions. Generally, the rules for direct examination require open-ended questions (e.g., "What did you see?" or "What happened next?"). Leading questions that suggest the answer or questions calling for a "yes" or "no" answer usually are not permitted (e.g., "Didn't the mother tell you that she hit the child with a belt?"). When testifying, caseworkers should:

- Be confident and self-assured;
- Listen carefully to the question and answer it directly;
- Ask that a question be repeated if it is difficult to hear or understand, but not make a habit of doing so;
- State facts, not opinions or conclusions (e.g., instead of saying that the mother was uncooperative and rude, state exactly what she said or did);
- State whether an answer is unknown or cannot be recalled;
- Speak clearly, distinctly, and loudly enough to be heard;
- Make eye contact with the questioner and the judge;
- Refer to the case file only as necessary in order to recall information.

When an attorney objects to a question or moves to strike an answer, the caseworker should wait until the judge rules on the motion before speaking. If the judge overrules the objection, then the caseworker should answer the question. If the judge sustains the objection, then the caseworker should not answer the question; the attorney will ask another one.

Cross-examination is questioning by attorneys other than the one who called the caseworker as a witness. The purpose of cross-examination is to expose weaknesses, errors, inconsistencies, biases, or other deficiencies in the testimony of the witness. The attorney also may focus on the caseworker's lack of experience or qualifications and will try to show that the caseworker did not do a thorough investigation or exercised poor judgment. Cross-examination can be unpleasant, but it is important that caseworkers not take it personally and remain outwardly calm, confident, and respectful. If a caseworker becomes hostile or defensive, the judge may discount the testimony.

Leading questions are permitted on cross-examination. Lawyers often will ask such questions, insist they be answered "yes" or ""no," and before the witness can explain, ask another question. When a "yes" or "no" requires an explanation, the witness can ask permission to explain the answer.

Ex Parte Communications

Ex parte communications are verbal or written communications addressed to the judge in a case by one party outside the presence of another party without copying the other party. They are strictly prohibited.[2] The prohibition extends to representatives of a party, including CPS caseworkers. Thus, caseworkers must never attempt to communicate privately with any judge about an open case; however, communications that are not case-specific, such as those suggested in Chapter 8, *Working with the Courts*, are not prohibited.

Children's Testimony

The courtroom can be an intimidating and traumatizing environment for most people, but especially for children, many of whom may be terrified by the prospect of testifying. They may become anxious or distraught. Some even freeze and are unable to respond to simple, preliminary questions. Younger children are more likely to have these types of reactions. Older children also are at risk of emotional trauma because they are more likely to be cross-examined aggressively by attorneys. For these reasons, children should not be called to testify, particularly against parents or relatives, unless the children's testimony is essential to proving critical allegations of the petitions or if the children want and need to testify for their own emotional well-being.

The Decision to Call a Child to Testify

Most child abuse or neglect cases can be proved by the testimony of other witnesses or by demonstrative or documentary evidence. In some cases, however, the child's testimony may be the only evidence. This is especially true of some sexual abuse cases.

The decision to call a child to testify should be made by CPS and its attorney, in consultation with the advocates and any therapists for the child. They need to weigh carefully the potential benefits of the child's testimony against the potential harm, both to the child from testifying and to the child, other family members, and the community if the charge is not proven.

Some CPS attorneys may not be sensitive to how a child can be affected by testifying. Consequently, the CPS caseworker (perhaps with the child's advocate and therapist) should be prepared to assert any concerns when deciding whether to call the child as a witness. It is critical that children never be put in a position of giving testimony against a parent or other caretaker unless they can be safeguarded against retaliation.

Every witness needs to be competent, which means that the witness must know the diff erence between the truth and a lie; appreciate the necessity of telling the truth; and be capable of observing, remembering, and describing events about which the witness will testify. This is a component of the *voir dire* process, a preliminary examination to determine competency of a witness or absence of bias of a juror. Under Federal law and that of many States, all witnesses are presumed competent, but some States have more restrictive requirements. If the issue is raised, the lawyers and judge may question the child to determine competency.

Younger children are more likely to not be allowed to testify due to lack of competency. T us, age is a significant factor in determining whether to call a child as a witness. The reliability and credibility of children's testimony has been the subject of much research, some of it contradictory. It can be summarized by saying that younger children are able to recall events less accurately and are more susceptible to suggestion.[3] A recommended approach for assessing children's ability to tell the truth is presented in Exhibit 7-1.

Credibility of a Child's Testimony

Decisions about children's credibility will depend mostly on their demeanor and the convincing force of their testimony. Other factors considered include whether the child's testimony is consistent with earlier statements or with any other credible evidence. The court also will be interested to know if there is any indication that the child has been coached or that the story is the result of intentional or unintentional influence by a parent, CPS, law enforcement, medical professionals, or others.

Care must be taken by all interviewers never to ask leading questions regarding possible abuse or neglect. Leading questions are those that suggest an answer, for example, "Didn't he grab your mother by the neck with his hands and choke her?" as opposed to "What did he do?" Any indication that the child's testimony may be the result of such suggestive questioning will undermine its credibility.

Likewise, repeated questioning of the child by the same or multiple persons, including professionals, about any abuse or neglect also will undermine credibility. CPS should have specially trained interviewers for children. CPS administrators are encouraged to develop protocols with police, prosecutors, medical personnel, and mental health treatment providers that minimize the number of interviews to which a child is subjected. Ideally, there should be only one interview, and it should occur in a safe, child-friendly environment. The interview should be videotaped to reduce the likelihood of subsequent interviews and to demonstrate that the interview was conducted appropriately.

Supporting Child Witnesses in the Courtroom

Supportive measures for young witnesses in child maltreatment proceedings might include videotaping depositions or allowing the child to speak to the judge in chambers, a common practice in child custody cases. Some States have relaxed hearsay rules for the statements of child witnesses and are more lenient in allowing leading questions of children.[4]

THE NATIONAL CHILDREN'S ADVOCACY CENTER

The National Children's Advocacy Center supports a network of community-based facilities that use a multidisciplinary team approach to respond to child abuse. The center is a resource for information about how to best conduct interviews of child victims and how to establish a model program. See Appendix B, *Resource Listings of Selected National Organizations Concerned With Child Maltreatment*.

EXHIBIT 7-1. ASSESSING YOUNGER CHILDREN'S ABILITY OR WILLINGNESS TO TELL THE TRUTH

- Begin the inquiry by establishing a rapport with the child. For example, ask about her age or favorite activity. Use this information to guide the inquiry.
- Ask the child the following:
  - What does it mean to tell the truth?
  - Why do you tell the truth? Is it important to tell the truth? Why?
  - What happens when you tell the truth?
  - What is a lie?
  - What have you told a lie about or when have you not told the truth?
  - What happens when you lie or do not tell the truth?
  - Are there times when it is OK to lie or not tell the truth? When?
- Using information provided by the child, ask questions and reframe the child's comments to assess her ability to discern the difference between a truth or a lie, as well as her willingness to tell the truth or to correct inaccurate information.
  - For example, if the child said she was 5 years old, begin the inquiry with "So, you're 7 years old?"
    - Assess if the child will correct the inaccurate statement. If the child agrees, respond by saying, "Oh, I thought you told me earlier that you were 5 years old?" Frequently, children will confi rm their original answer.
    - In this situation, ask the child if the statement that she is 7 years old is a lie or the truth. Explain to the child that if information is not correct, you want them to provide the truth or correct answer and that they must be sure to do this in any situation, including court testimony.
  - Another example would be, if the interviewer is wearing black shoes, to ask the child, "If I told you my shoes were yellow, would that be the truth or a lie?" Alternatively, "If I told you that my shoes were black, would that be the truth or a lie?"

Proceed with similar questions or statements that will help with the assessment.

- Conclude the inquiry by praising the child for his participation and affirmative answers. Stress the importance of telling the truth in court.
- When a child needs to testify, the CPS caseworker must decide whether utilizing one of these measures would benefit the child and facilitate the testimony. If so, the caseworker should confer with the CPS attorney in advance of the trial to file the necessary motions, to develop the required supporting evidence, and to make arrangements for whatever equipment may be required if the motion is granted.

Taking frequent breaks and making the setting less formal are other measures a court can take to make children more comfortable in the courtroom and to facilitate their testimony. The judges can come off the bench, sit at the same level as the children and other participants, or not wear judicial robes. Some casual conversation with children can help relax them, as will excluding unnecessary participants from the courtroom. Permitting very young children to sit on the lap of a support person while testifying is another possibility. Some judges will take or authorize these measures on their own initiative, while others may need to be asked or encouraged to do so.

A child witness should not enter the courtroom until it is time to testify and should be prepared in advance for that moment and what will happen after. There will be people present in the courtroom whom the child has never seen, often including an armed bailiff . The child will be the center of attention, which may create or heighten anxiety or fear. CPS caseworkers (or the CPS agency attorney) should do what they can to prepare the child for this experience. At minimum, preparation should include visiting the courtroom when it is not in use, practicing being sworn in, sitting in the witness stand and answering questions (unrelated to the case), speaking into the microphone, and seeing the view from the bench. Tell the child who will be present, and point out where each of those individuals will sit.

The CPS caseworker or attorney should familiarize the child with the court process, including:

- Explaining that different lawyers will ask questions and giving examples;
- Describing objections and explaining how the child should wait until the judge rules on them;
- Explaining the terms "sustained" and "overruled;"
- Role playing the competency inquiry (without telling the child the answers);
- Arranging for the child to meet with the CPS attorney (if this meeting has not yet occurred) and assisting the attorney and child so that they may interact comfortably.

While it is inappropriate to remind a child what to say or otherwise attempt to infl uence the child's testimony, it may be appropriate for the caseworker and attorney to review with the child any videotaped, audiotaped, or written statement that may have been made.

The advocates are particularly helpful allies in cases where children will testify. The GAL or CASA often may have a closer personal relationship with the child than others involved in the case and be in a better position to facilitate the child's ability to testify effectively.

Standards for Testifying by Alternative Means

Many States have passed laws regarding child witnesses in the courtroom. These laws focus primarily on protecting a child from having to testify in the presence of the alleged abuser. One protective measure is the use of closed-circuit television in which the child's testimony is broadcast into the courtroom where the judge, jury, and defendant can see and hear what the child says. The lawyers are present with the child, and the defendant's lawyers can cross-examine the child while communicating privately with their client. This approach will be deemed constitutional regarding the right to face one's accuser, provided there is sufficient evidence for the judge to find that the child would be significantly traumatized by the presence of the defendant and, thus, unable to testify.[5] Expert testimony may be necessary to establish the basis for a request to protect a child in this way.

EXHIBIT 7-2. CHILD TESTIMONY

In noncriminal proceedings, such as child maltreatment cases, standards for child testimony are less rigorous. These differences are best demonstrated by reference to Section 5 of the Uniform Child Witness Testimony by Alternative Methods Act, entitled Standards for Determining Whether Child Witness May Testify by Alternative Method, which states:

(a) In a criminal proceeding, the presiding officer may allow a child witness to testify by an alternative method only in the following situations:

1. The child may testify otherwise than in an open forum in the presence and full view of the finder of fact if the presiding officer finds by clear and convincing evidence that the child would suffer serious emotional trauma that would substantially impair the child's ability to communicate with the finder of fact if required to testify in the open forum.
2. The child may testify other than face-to-face with the defendant if the presiding officer finds by clear and convincing evidence that the child would suffer serious emotional trauma that would substantially impair the child's ability to communicate with the finder of fact if required to be confronted face-to-face by the defendant.

(b) In a noncriminal proceeding, the presiding officer may allow a child witness to testify by an alternative method if the presiding officer finds by a preponderance of the evidence that allowing the child to testify by an alternative method is necessary to serve the best interests of the child or enable the child to communicate with the finder of fact. In making this finding, the presiding officer shall consider:

1. The nature of the proceeding;
2. The age and maturity of the child;
3. The relationship of the child to the parties in the proceeding;
   a. The nature and degree of emotional trauma that the child may suffer in testifying;

Any other relevant factor, such as developmental delays.[9]

The most significant recent development regarding the testimony of child witnesses is the adoption of the Uniform Child Witness Testimony by Alternative Methods Act, drafted by the National Conference of Commissioners on Uniform State Laws and approved and recommended for enactment in all States.[6] In 2003, the American Bar Association approved the law. At the time of this report's publication, three States had adopted it, and two more had legislation pending.[7] The Act applies to children under 13 years of age and to both criminal (including juvenile delinquency) and non-criminal proceedings. It establishes standards for determining whether a child witness may testify by alternative means.[8]

The Act also prescribes the content of the court's order and requires a full and fair opportunity to cross- examine the child witness. It does not dictate the alternative methods for receiving a child's testimony, but strongly suggests that only two current practices are likely to satisfy all provisions of the Act: closed- circuit television and courtroom arrangements that avoid direct confrontation between a witness and a particular party or the finder of fact.[10] See Exhibit 7-2 for more information about the Act.

JUDGES' EXPECTATIONS OF CHILD PROTECTIVE SERVICES CASEWORKERS

Judges and CPS caseworkers generally do not have routine, direct contact with one another. Communication typically occurs in the courtroom and often is transmitted via CPS or the parents' attorneys. Judges may ask a question or make a request directly to caseworkers, but there is limited opportunity for caseworkers to become familiar with them. Many judges, however, are receptive to enhancing their relationships and to ensuring a positive experience for individuals who appear in their courtroom. CPS caseworkers can improve these relationships through improved awareness of courtroom rules, procedures, expectations, and the personalities of those involved.

Judges expect that CPS caseworkers will successfully:

- Engage clients in the court process;
- Work effectively with others;
- Arrive on time;
- Know the law and follow court rules;
- Prepare appropriate court orders.

Fulfilling these expectations, as described below, will help improve caseworkers' court experiences.

Engaging Clients in the Court Process

The foundation for effective casework is the relationship between the caseworker and the client. Some clients are less appealing than others or are more difficult to engage. Some caseworkers' experiences or personalities equip them to perform this aspect of the work better than others. Regardless of these variables, engaging clients at the outset is one of the keys to successful outcomes and requires sincerely communicating concern for them and their children as well as a desire that the family be together. Caseworkers should be empathetic and sensitive to clients' feelings and needs and should take an approach that identifi es the specific strengths of each client and that tailors interventions to those strengths. Caseworkers also should engage parents as a means of encouraging, motivating, and inspiring them to take the necessary steps to retain or to regain custody of their children. Caseworkers who experience the most success with families are the ones who work most effectively with parents. Insightful judges recognize this quality in caseworkers and value the results it produces.

Communication with the clients must be direct, honest, and unambiguous to avoid any misunderstanding of important information, including conveying possible case outcomes. Before the hearing, an explanation of the court process will give the parents some idea of what to expect. After the hearing, the caseworker should help parents understand key decisions, reinforce the outcome and expectations, and answer questions. Parents often leave the courtroom not knowing what happened or why, what will happen next, or what is expected of them. It is easy for those who are familiar with the court hearings, the terminology, and the consequences of a judge's decisions to forget how foreign the experience may be to others.

Most States require case and service plans to be incorporated into the court records for the judge to determine if they meet requirements regarding services and reunification efforts. In fact, discussion of the agency's actions and the parents' progress toward their goals comprises the largest part of the hearings. During testimony and in the documents, caseworkers should focus on the most serious issues that must be resolved to achieve reunification. (See Chapter 4, *The Juvenile Court Process*, for more information about developing case plans.) Since the judge often will ask how the caseworker dealt with these issues, it should be documented that the caseworker:

- Made clear what the client needs to change and how;
- Identified and built on the clients' strengths and those of the extended family;
- Offered whatever services and resources were needed;
- Rewarded the clients' successes and encouraged further progress;
- Advocated for the client with CPS supervisors, service providers, and the court;
- Took care not to demand more of clients than was realistically possible due to limitations of time, transportation, resources, other responsibilities, or innate abilities.

Working Effectively with Others

Another critical skill for caseworkers is the ability to establish good working relationships with others, including service providers, throughout the legal process. Some communities have multidisciplinary team meetings to discuss cases, particularly complex ones, which may involve experts who have no direct involvement with the case. Other communities commonly have "staffings" at which all service providers and those involved in the court process meet to discuss a case and to strategize ways to address the needs presented.

Whether or not these structures are in place, resolving child maltreatment cases successfully almost invariably involves a team approach, with the caseworker both the coach and a key member of the team. Success often will depend on the caseworker's collaboration skills or ability to cooperate with the other team members, particularly the child's advocates and the parents' attorneys. Working effectively means:

- Treating the other team members with respect;
- Involving them in identifying the issues the case presents;
- Thinking collectively about how to resolve those issues;
- Sharing information;
- Communicating about new developments as they arise.

Establishing good working relationships within the team is more likely to result in positive case outcomes. As working relationships become more effective, conflicts will be less likely, and future interactions in other cases will be more constructive. Judges appreciate the efforts of caseworkers who facilitate constructive interactions and achieve consensus on course of cases.

In some cases, service providers may have to testify about the services and the families; therefore, it is important for caseworkers to establish good relationships with them. Judges may have questions for the caseworker about the service providers, so caseworkers will want to make personal contacts with them to understand what they do, whom they serve, and their criteria for providing services and to determine the quality of their work. Service providers also should be participants in team discussions about the case.

Similarly, a good relationship between CPS and the public mental health agency is important. Unfortunately, this relationship can be acrimonious in many communities. If CPS depends on the mental health agency to perform evaluations or to provide treatment or placements, including hospitalization, CPS should take the initiative to establish a good working relationship between the two agencies. Defining each agency's responsibilities, setting timelines for completion of evaluations or other tasks, and establishing lines of communication for sharing information are just a few of the issues that need to be addressed. Discussion of these issues should involve the heads of each agency and the court. Individual caseworkers, however, can contribute to this process by identifying problems that arise between the agencies in specific cases and documenting how those problems affected the child or CPS's ability to comply with timelines established by the Adoption and Safe Families Act (ASFA) (P.L. 105–89). Sharing that information with supervisors might lead to the initiation of a process to improve communication and cooperation between the agencies. In the absence of such a process, the relationship between the caseworker and a mental health counterpart can produce good results, even in a flawed system. The ability to access quality services on a timely basis distinguishes caseworkers in the eyes of judges.

Arriving on Time

Some judges are habitually late, while others are always on time. All of them, however, will expect timeliness from caseworkers in the performance of their duties, including:

- Attending court hearings;
- Filing court reports;
- Following up on the requirements of court orders;
- Transferring cases between caseworkers;
- Keeping cases on track for resolution within the ASFA timelines.

Knowing the Law and Following Court Rules

Agency and court practices and procedures in child maltreatment cases must comply with Federal and State laws. It is essential, therefore, that caseworkers have good knowledge and understanding of the key principles, mandates, and purposes of these laws.

Many courts have rules governing the filing of court reports, discovery, distribution of experts' evaluations, continuances or postponements, notice of placement changes, notice of hearings, and conduct of hearings. Caseworkers will be expected to know these rules and to abide by them. They also should expect others in the process to do likewise and, when they do not, should notify the CPS attorney.

Preparing Court Orders

Court orders in child maltreatment cases should be prepared at the conclusion of the hearings, then distributed to the parties and other participants. They are more accurate and complete if written or dictated while the court's decisions and directives are fresh in the minds of all participants. Any disagreements or misunderstandings can be resolved immediately, and the parents can depart with a written statement of the court's expectations of them and of CPS.

Orders need to be clear and easy to understand. The use of forms is essential, and a clerk, a lawyer, or the judge can complete them. For ease of understanding and distribution of sufficient copies, it is preferable that they be prepared on a computer and printer in the courtroom. Objections to this approach are based on the time it takes to discuss and prepare the orders. Nevertheless, it will save time that often is spent debating and clarifying what the court ordered. Lack of technology may be an impediment in some courts, so this approach to order preparation is not yet common. Where it is implemented, it contributes significantly to improved understanding and outcomes. CPS can encourage courts, and perhaps assist them with necessary hardware, to implement this practice.

End Notes

[1] *Daubert v. Merrell Dow Pharmaceuticals, Inc.*, 509 U.S. 579 (1993); *Kumho Tire Co. v. Carmichael*, 526 U.S. 137 (1999); *General Electric Co. v. Joiner*, 522 U.S. 136 (1997).

[2] American Bar Association. (1999a). *ABA Model Code of Judicial Conduct*, Canon 3B(7). Chicago, IL: Author.

[3] Sagatun, I. J., & Edwards, L. P. (Eds.). (1995). Expert witnesses in child abuse cases. In *Child abuse and the legal system* (pp. 209–228). Chicago, IL: Nelson-Hall; Ceci, S., & Bruck, M. (1995). *Jeopardy in the courtroom.* Washington, DC: American Psychological Association; Poole, D., & Lamb, M. (1999). *Investigative interviews of children.* Washington, DC: American Psychological Association; Walker, A. G. (1999). *Questioning of children: A linguistic perspective.* Washington, DC: American Bar Association; Ceci, S. J., & Bruck, M. (2000). Why judges must insist on electronically preserved recordings of child interviews. *Court Review, 2*, 10–12; Crossman, A. M., Powell, M. B., Principe, G. F., & Ceci, S. J. (2002). Child testimony in custody cases: A review. *Journal of Forensic Psychology Practice, 2*(1), 1–31.

[4] *Idaho v. Wright*, 497 U.S. 805 (1990).

[5] *Iowa v. Coy*, 487 U.S. 1012 (1988); *Maryland v. Craig*, 497 U.S. 836 (1990).

[6] National Conference of Commissioners on Uniform State Laws. (2002).

[7] National Conference of Commissioners on Uniform State Laws. (2005). *Child Witness Testimony by Alternative Methods Act* [On-line]. Available: *http:// www.nccusl.org/Update/ ActSearchResults.aspx.*

[8] *Iowa v. Coy*, 487 U.S. 1012 (1988); *Maryland v. Craig*, 497 U.S. 836 (1990).

[9] National Conference of Commissioners on Uniform State Laws. (2002).

[10] National Conference of Commissioners on Uniform State Laws. (2002).

In: Working with the Courts in Child Protection ISBN: 978-1-61668-303-0
Editors: Raymond T. Devon

Chapter 8

WORKING WITH THE COURTS

Just as judges have power to initiate improvements in court practice and performance, they also can be formidable roadblocks to such improvements. Some judges may be intentional in their determination to continue operating in familiar ways; others simply may be unaware of alternatives, their power to make changes, or the resources that are available to inform and to support efforts to improve court operations. The ability of child protective services (CPS) and of individual caseworkers to improve the court process depends on their understanding judges and knowing how to work with them, to support them, and to provide them with the information and tools they need to do their job better. This chapter deals with measures agencies and individual caseworkers can pursue.

UNDERSTANDING JUDGES

Almost all judges are lawyers. Most are politicians who had to win election or were appointed through a process that was at least partly political. Judges vary widely in terms of their values, experience, intelligence, skills, knowledge, work ethic, receptivity to change, and personalities, but like other lawyers, many tend to be analytical thinkers. Judges focus on facts and look for cases that are presented, or problems addressed, in logical progression. They expect witnesses to answer questions directly, and they want people who testify or make oral presentations to "get to the point" and to express themselves succinctly. Most are practical and decisive, and nearly all are impatient to some degree, particularly with delays, poor performance, dramatic behavior, and excessive detail.

Judges' personalities are revealed over time, as are their work habits, knowledge, skills, commitment to doing the work well, and their proclivities regarding particular issues or circumstances. Caseworkers who appear regularly in the juvenile court will learn quickly which judges are the easiest and hardest to work with and which ones are most likely to be receptive to improving court practice.

In some States, judges are elected or appointed to the juvenile court bench and sit only in that court. In most States, however, the juvenile court is part of a larger court system. In these jurisdictions, judges occasionally may remain in the juvenile court assignment for extended periods of time, but the most common practice is for judges to be assigned to that court on a periodic rotation. The length of the assignment may vary from as little as 1 day to as much as a few years. Generally, 3 to 5 years is considered optimal because it takes time to learn about the laws governing the court's proceedings; the complexities and dynamics of child maltreatment; the availability and quality of the services, resources, and interventions at the court's disposal; the administrative responsibilities of the role; and the myriad professionals who appear before the court.[1]

This is particularly true for the majority of judges who had no juvenile court experience as lawyers.

Ideally, judges and judicial officers will be assigned to the juvenile court only after substantial training on the unique responsibilities of a judge in that court, the problems and needs of the court's clientele, and the human services systems on which it relies. Court improvements are less likely to occur without the leadership and the support of a knowledgeable and experienced judge. Indeed, some States have extensive training programs for both new and experienced juvenile court judges and formal certification procedures to ensure that they are well- prepared for the difficult work of that court. Much of the knowledge that juvenile court judges acquire, however, is gained by sitting in the juvenile court on a consistent basis over a significant period of time.

WHAT CASEWORKERS CAN DO TO EFFECT CHANGE IN THE COURT

CPS caseworkers who practice in a court that has good judicial leadership are encouraged to find ways to participate in the collaborative efforts underway in the work of that court. Doing so will enhance their knowledge and enrich their work experience. Of course, some judges are friendlier and more approachable than others, and some will be more receptive to suggestions than others. Judges are more likely to respond to an individual caseworker's suggestion if the caseworker has established credibility and earned the judge's respect by the quality of her performance in individual cases. Some judges also may respond more favorably if approached by a caseworker who is accompanied by a child's advocate or a parent's attorney, so the caseworker is not suspected of seeking favored treatment.

Interacting and Building Positive Working Relationships with Judges

In taking steps to build positive working relationships with judges, CPS caseworkers can:

- Introduce themselves to the judge at each court appearance or other encounter; Speak and write as clearly and plainly as possible;
- Be concise and to the point;
- Learn as much as possible about the judge's tendencies, personality, and likes and dislikes and be guided by that knowledge;
- Determine the history of the judge's interactions with CPS and how it may affect the judge's handling of particular issues or dealings with caseworkers;
- Build relationships with clerks, bailiff s, and court reporters;
- Follow local practices and protocols regarding appropriate dress for the courtroom, for addressing the court, and approaching the bench;
- Be polite and respectful, but when the opportunity presents itself, do not hesitate to assert strongly held opinions about what the judge should order or decide in regard to a case;
- Not display emotion, especially anger or disdain, if the judge makes a decision with which CPS or the caseworker disagrees.

JUDICIAL TRAINING PROGRAMS

Numerous training programs for juvenile court judges who hear child maltreatment cases are available at locations through the National Council of Juvenile and Family Court Judges (NCJFCJ) and other legal, judicial, and social services organizations. Judges interested in improving court practices and their own knowledge and skills can be referred to those organizations a nearby lead judge in one of the 25 NCJFCJ model court sites across the country. NCJFCJ, the National Center for State Courts, the American Bar Association's Center on Children and the Law, and the Youth Law Center also are excellent sources of information about child maltreatment litigation. (See Appendix B, *Resource Listings of Selected National Organizations Concerned With Child Maltreatment*, for more information on these organizations.)

Effecting Change in the Court

Judges often are perceived as omnipotent, and the idea that CPS, much less an individual caseworker, could infl uence them to change practice may seem fanciful. Indeed, some judges are impervious to change, regardless of the source of the suggestion or the pressure to do so. Many others, however, understand that good outcomes in child maltreatment cases require the cooperative efforts of CPS, service providers, and the court. In several urban and small communities, judges meet regularly with CPS representatives to improve procedures, policies, and practices, and to enhance services. The State Court Improvement Program and the National Council of Juvenile and Family Court Judges (NCJFCJ) Model Court Project have contributed to this development. (See Chapter 9, *Court Improvement and Best Practices*, for more information on these important initiatives.)

For those child maltreatment courts that lack strong judicial leadership, the following list offers suggestions for informing and motivating promising juvenile court judges to take leadership in constructive ways:

- Provide information about particular "best practices" that could constitute significant improvement in how the court operates. Offer to help plan and implement the practice locally or to set up a meeting of stakeholders to discuss it.

- Invite the judge to make a presentation at a training for CPS caseworkers on a topic that the judge knows well. Preparing a presentation can be a good learning experience, particularly if the judge is provided with good resource materials for that purpose.
- Recognize the judge's accomplishments in some way that does not appear to be currying favor but, instead, may be motivational. Joining with child and parent advocates for this purpose would lessen any appearance of impropriety. A Child Abuse Prevention Month event might be a good opportunity to honor a judge.
- Devise a strategy for motivating the judge to endorse the development of a mission and goals statement by a multidisciplinary group if the court has none. Do the same if the court has no rules that govern procedures or if they need to be updated.
- Suggest the development of model templates for court reports, reports on reasonable efforts, mental health assessment referrals, child support referrals, and other common forms.
- Invite a judge on a ride-along to observe the realities of being a CPS caseworker on the frontline. The judge should not be assigned to a case resulting from anyone observed during the ride-along.
- Make the judge aware of caseload demands, time constraints, and resource and service deficits.
- Ask judges to support CPS's budget request in States where judges are not precluded from such activities.
- Suggest a training event and secure the judge's endorsement. Invite the judge to help plan it, and elicit the judge's suggestions for topics. Ask the judge to make a presentation, and involve a multidisciplinary group to design the training, secure presenters, and arrange for a site. Encourage State judicial educators to address topics of particular importance at their periodic judicial training events and then encourage a local judge to attend.
- Keep informed of local, State, and national grant opportunities. The State Court Improvement Program is perhaps the best such opportunity. Collaborating on a grant application can be a very good learning experience that promotes understanding and strengthens working relationships, even if a grant is not awarded.
- Suggest that an ad hoc, multidisciplinary committee be formed to consider implementation of some of the recommendations of:

    - *Emerging Practices in the Prevention of Child Abuse and Neglect* at *Adoption and Permanency Guidelines: Improving Court Practice in Child Abuse and Neglect Cases* at www.ncjfcj.org or http:// www.pppncjfcj.org;
    - *Resource Guidelines: Improving Court Practice in Child Abuse and Neglect Cases* http:// www.pppncjfcj.org/html/ publications. html.
    - *About the Pew Commission on Children in Foster Care at* http://pewfostercare.org/ about.
- Promote the creation of a multidisciplinary child abuse and neglect committee that can identify problems devise and implement solutions.
- Identify needed, but insufficient or nonexistent, services and enlist the judge's assistance in securing or developing them. Examples might be a visitation center, a program for child observers of domestic violence, or a parenting course specifically for fathers with a history of violence toward their child's mother.
- Provide the court with periodic reports on the status of its cases.

Some of these suggestions may be undertaken by individual caseworkers; others may require involvement by CPS lawyers or administrators, depending on the size of the community and the culture of the court and CPS.

CPS caseworkers also may direct judges to valuable resources. For example, they can provide the judge with literature regarding judicial training from the NCJFCJ, the ABA Center on Children and the Law, the National Center for State Courts, and the National Association of Counsel for Children.

Similarly, caseworkers may refer judges who are interested in improving court practices and enhancing their own knowledge and skills to the above-referenced organizations for publications and technical assistance.

They also can be referred for technical assistance to a nearby lead judge in one of the 25 model court sites across the country or to a State Court Improvement Project judge who has effectively addressed particular issues. Other valuable sources of training, information, and technical assistance sponsored by the Children's Bureau are the eight National Resource Centers, including one on legal and judicial issues, two clearinghouses, and four Technical Assistance Support Systems. (See Appendix B, *Resource Listings of Selected National Organizations Concerned with Child Maltreatment*, for more information on these organizations.)

Working with Problem Judges

Unfortunately, there are judges who are verbally abusive; unreasonably demanding; habitually late starting court, preparing orders, or reading reports; biased; or incompetent. If a pattern of any of these behaviors or some other significant deficit is identified in multiple cases by more than one caseworker, the caseworker or CPS should not feel powerless. Caseworkers should request assistance from CPS administrators and attorneys when confronting challenging judges. Actions that can be taken to address such problem behaviors include:

- Asking the CPS attorney, supervisor, or administrator to speak to the judge on behalf of CPS or the caseworkers or to file a complaint with the State's Judicial Standards Commission, depending on the nature of the problem behavior;
- Speaking out in any reappointment, retention, or re-election process in which the judge must participate, as well as identifying and encouraging alternative candidates. Joining with children's advocates or parents' attorneys would make these suggested actions more credible than if they come just from CPS.[2]

There is the risk with each of these strategies, however, that nothing will change and that the judge will be vindictive toward CPS or the caseworkers. Legitimate complaints must nevertheless be voiced because it is quite common for problem judges to be reassigned or not to be retained or re-elected when well-documented grievances are made known to authorities or the public.

End Notes

[1] Edwards, L. P. (1992). The juvenile court and the role of the juvenile court judge. *Juvenile and Family Court Journal, 42*(2), 30–32.

[2] American Bar Association. (1999b). *ABA Model Code of Judicial Conduct*, Canon 3B(4), 3B(5) and Commentary, 3B(6). Chicago, IL: Author.

In: Working with the Courts in Child Protection ISBN: 978-1-61668-303-0
Editors: Raymond T. Devon

Chapter 9

COURT IMPROVEMENT AND BEST PRACTICES

An integrated and comprehensive approach to the complex problems of families involved with child protective services (CPS) and the courts is critical to achieving safety and permanency for children. Evolving Federal child welfare legislation has prompted CPS and the courts to implement innovative policy and programmatic changes. T us, the pioneering efforts of court and child advocates have created a variety of inventive practices focused on accomplishing positive outcomes for families. This chapter provides an overview of the Child and Family Services Reviews (CFSRs) and the courts and information about best practices and model court programs existing throughout the country. It also provides information about the importance of judicial leadership in improving court practice.

CHILD AND FAMILY SERVICES REVIEWS AND THE COURTS

The Federal CFSR process is a results-oriented, comprehensive monitoring and review system designed to assist States in improving safety, permanency, and well-being outcomes for children and families who come into contact with the nation's public child welfare systems.[1] Fiscal sanctions may result from failure to meet the measures of the CFSRs, but it is the State's desire to improve practice and outcomes for the nation's most vulnerable children that has motivated States to work on comprehensive Program

Improvement Plans (PIP) to correct the weaknesses and gaps identified in the CFSR.[2]

Although CPS and related child welfare agencies are the primary focus of the CFSR and PIP, there is a clear need for collaboration with the courts for the following reasons:

- CPS performance depends, in part, on its relationship with the courts and on court performance;
- CPS can use the legal system to learn how to overcome legal barriers that diminish its performance;
- CPS and the courts have mutual goals for achieving child welfare outcomes, especially in the area of achieving permanency;
- Court reform requires CPS and other key stakeholders' involvement;
- CPS has an interest in ensuring that the courts carry out PIP goals.[3]

The CSFRs evaluate CPS performance based partly on how well it works with the courts and other agencies to achieve child welfare outcomes, such as the time in care until adoption or reunification. CPS collaboration with the courts also may help overcome or mitigate court-related barriers to achieving CFSR outcomes. For instance, courts may provide CPS with strategies to work with Federal and State confidentiality requirements in order to obtain complete information about an abused child's family, which may result in an improved safety outcome for the child.[4] The roles of CPS and the courts and their methods for achieving these mutual goals are most efficient and productive when a uniform, long-range plan and a cooperative relationship are established.[5]

Additionally, each State's Court Improvement Program (CIP) (discussed later in the chapter) is expected to help achieve PIP goals.[6] The juvenile and family courts cannot effectively perform their child welfare responsibilities in isolation; CPS participation is an essential part of court reform. Specific improvements, such as strengthening case management and information systems for recording a child's court and placement history, require collaboration.[7]

Using the CFSRs as a catalyst, CPS can either initiate or improve upon an already existing collaborative relationship with the State juvenile and family courts in several ways, including:

- Research other States' CFSR processes, including how they collaborate with their legal system to improve their CFSR performance;
- Consider all legal and judicial issues suggested by the CFSR performance indicators, which can be prepared with the aid of the State's legal system;
- Invite the juvenile and family court judges and legal professionals to participate in meetings to plan and to organize the State's CFSR process;
- Explain the importance of the CFSR to juvenile and family court judges and legal professionals and persuade them to participate in the CFSR process;
- Include juvenile and family court judges and legal professionals in PIP development;
- Explain to the court, legislature, and caseworkers what resources are required for successful development and implementation of the PIP.[8]

Once CPS and the courts begin working together, they can tackle systemic problems affecting child safety, well-being, and permanency more efficiently. The agency can suggest improvements that may help courts make better decisions for children, such as:

- Improving agency court reports and testimony;
- Upgrading legal representation of the agency;
- Assisting judges to implement the Adoption and Safe Families Act (ASFA) and its regulations;
- Helping courts obtain better performance data or providing them with helpful data;
- Getting caseworkers to attend court hearings more consistently;
- Working together to improve court resources;
- Improving State law to ensure better and timelier services for families, thereby making it easier for judges to deliver timely decisions.[9]

These changes could help eliminate barriers the courts face, such as insufficient information, the length of time needed to resolve permanency issues, slow progress in cases, and obstacles to timely termination of parental rights. Their implementation can aid both the courts and the agencies in achieving better outcomes for children and families.[10] For more on how and why agencies should work with the courts, see Appendix E, *Legal and Judicial Issues Suggested By The Child And Family Services Review Performance Indicators.*

PEW COMMISSION ON CHILDREN IN FOSTER CARE

The Pew Commission on Children in Foster Care was established to develop recommendations to improve outcomes for children in the foster care system. Of primary importance are expediting the movement of children from foster care into safe, permanent, and nurturing families and preventing unnecessary placements in foster care.[11] The Commission recognized that while dependency courts and child welfare agencies both work to protect children, too often they work in isolation. To address these problems, the Commission released a set of recommendations focused on reforming Federal fi nancing and court oversight of foster care, including court and agency collaboration.[12]

Several key recommendations highlighted the need for effective collaboration to promote the protection and well-being of children:

- The U.S. Department of Health and Human Services (HHS) should require that the State IV-E plans, PIPs, and CIPs demonstrate effective collaboration;
- HHS should require States to establish commissions on children in foster care, ideally co-directed by the State's child welfare agency director and Chief Justice;
- Congress should appropriate $10 million to train court personnel, a portion of which should be used for joint training of child welfare agency staff and court personnel;
- Local and State courts and agencies should collaborate and plan for the collection and sharing of all relevant data and information that can aid in making better decisions and creating better outcomes for children.[13]

The Commission's report states, "Collaboration should recognize that the children and families involved with the child welfare system are often simultaneously engaged with other community agencies and services—schools, health care, mental health, child care, and others. Children and families are better served when these multiple community partners come together on their behalf." [14] Following their release, a number of national and State child welfare organizations and judicial entities issued resolutions supporting the recommendations. These organizations and entities included the National Council of Juvenile and Family Court Judges (NCJFCJ), the Conference of Chief Justices and Conference of State Court Administrators, the North American Council on Adoptable Children, the Judicial Council of California, and the Texas Supreme Court Task Force on Foster Care.[15]

BEST PRACTICES

Legislative changes and CPS and judicial efforts are actualized through the daily practices of court personnel and CPS caseworkers. These practices need to incorporate proven methods that are responsive to the individual and multiple needs of families who are linked to different and complex systems. Many judges and others in the courts recognize the importance of collaborating with other systems to implement creative approaches that best serve families. The following are initiatives and legislation designed to promote the use of best practices in this area.

The State CIP

The State CIP provides grants to State courts "...to conduct assessments of their foster care and adoption laws and judicial processes and to develop and implement a plan for system improvement."[16] The CIP was first authorized as part of the Omnibus Budget Reconciliation Act of 1993 (P.L. 103–66, sections 13711–13712) and was first reauthorized by ASFA (P.L. 105–89) of 1997 without substantial programmatic changes. The CIP is a Federal grant program designed to improve the quality of court proceedings in handling child abuse and neglect cases. Federal funding goes to the highest court of each State, which administers the funds and directs the project. Each State has wide discretion on how to use CIP funds, but they must be used to improve the litigation process for abused and neglected children. The program was reauthorized again in 2002 by the Promoting Safe and Stable Families Amendments of 2001 (P.L. 107–133). This reauthorization expanded the program's scope to include the implementation of a PIP, as necessary, in response to findings identified in a CFSR. Through CIP, all State court systems are required to participate in the implementation of a CFSR PIP when a State court system is involved.[17]

NEW CIP GRANTS[18]

In the Deficit Reduction Act of 2005 (DRA), Congress expanded the CIP to authorize two new grants. The new grants include:

- A data collection and analysis grant to help ensure that foster children's needs for safety, permanency, and well-being are met in a timely and complete manner;
- A grant for training judges, attorneys, and other legal personnel in child welfare cases and conducting cross-training with child welfare agency staff and contractors.

These new grants are authorized for $10 million each for fi ve years.

The DRA also establishes the following important new collaboration requirements for both State courts and child welfare agencies:

- The law requires State court applicants to include in their applications for all three CIP grants a demonstration of meaningful and ongoing collaboration among the courts in the State, the State child welfare agency (or any other agency with which the State contracts to administer Titles IV-B or IV-E), and, where applicable, Indian Tribes.
- The law adds a Title IV-B State plan requirement for the State or Tribal child welfare agency to demonstrate substantial, ongoing, and meaningful collaboration with State courts in the development and implementation of its State plans under Titles IV-B and IV-E, as well as PIPs developed as a result of the Child and Family Services and IV-E Foster Care Eligibility Reviews.

The Model Courts Project

The Permanency Planning for Children Department (PPCD) of NCJFCJ established the Child Victims Act Model Court Project in 1992 with funding from the Office of Juvenile Justice and Delinquency Prevention.[19] There are 25 model courts across the country, including those in New York, Los

Angeles, and Chicago, as well as smaller communities such as Zuni, New Mexico, the site of a Tribal court. These courts and their community partners, including CPS, work with PPCD and each other to improve court practice in child abuse and neglect cases. They identify barriers to permanency and other successful outcomes for children in their court and social services systems and develop and implement strategies for overcoming those barriers. Annual status reports outlining the goals and accomplishments of each of these communities are available from PPCD at http:// www.ncjfcj.org/content/ view/81/145/ and are an excellent starting point for identifying successful resolutions of problems encountered by judges and CPS personnel.

TRIBAL COURTS

Prior to the passage of the Indian Child Welfare Act (ICWA) of 1978, private, State, and Federal agencies typically removed abused and neglected Indian children from their families and Tribal communities. Often, these children were placed without considering the cultural and other effects this would have on them.[20] State courts often ignored the sovereign authority of Tribal courts with regard to these children.

With ICWA, child welfare proceedings involving Indian children are treated differently from other child welfare cases. If the child lives on a reservation, the case must be decided by the Tribal courts of the child's Tribe instead of by State courts. Many cases involving Indian children who do not live on a reservation can be transferred to Tribal courts. These children, must be enrolled as members of an Indian Tribe or eligible for membership and have a biological parent who is a Tribe member.

When foster care placements or termination of parental rights proceedings for Indian children are brought before the State courts, those children, their Native American custodians, and their Tribes have the right to become involved, enabling the cases to be transferred to Indian Tribal courts. The children's parents, Indian custodians, and the Tribes also are entitled to a notice of the State court action, so they can appear and respond to the charges or intervene and request a transfer, if appropriate.

In 1990, Congress enacted the Indian Child Protection and Family Violence Act (P.L. 101–630). Among other things, it authorizes Federal funds to be used by the Bureau of Indian Affairs for a variety of purposes, including to help Tribes establish CPS programs and develop multidisciplinary child abuse investigation and prosecution teams.[21]

The Strengthening Abuse and Neglect Courts Act

In FY2001, Congress enacted the Strengthening Abuse and Neglect Courts Act (SANCA) (P.L. 106–314) and funded it for the first time in FY 2002. The purpose of SANCA is to award grants to State and local courts to enable them to develop and to implement automated data collection and case-tracking systems so that they can eventually use such systems to evaluate court performance. To date, grants have been made to six States (Colorado, Florida, Georgia, Idaho, New Jersey, and Oregon) to pilot the implementation of suggested performance measures developed by the American Bar Association, NCJFCJ, and the National Center for State Courts. http://www.ncsconline.org/WC/Publications/KIS_ Fam JusSANCAProject. pdf for an overview. The Act makes financial resources available to qualifying courts "... for the purpose of developing, implementing and maintaining automated information systems that enable the nation's abuse and neglect courts to effectively and efficiently meet the intended goals of the Adoption and Safe Families Act." Courts that apply must have "...a demonstrated history of collaborative planning and court improvement..." and "must have full support from [their] collaborative partners," including CPS.[22]

The Toolkit Project

In FY 2003, the Children's Bureau funded a project to help courts develop a viable approach to engaging in continuous quality improvement with regard to the handling of dependency cases. The American Bar Association, the National Center for State Courts, and the NCJFCJ are working together to help courts improve their performance by addressing the two most critical and challenging areas of court reform: court performance measurement and judicial workload. Utilizing a guide and toolkit recently developed by these organizations under a grant from the David and Lucile Packard Foundation, the groups are providing targeted technical assistance to help six project courts achieve increased accountability and better performance. The final products of this project will be an updated guidebook and toolkit that will provide revised instrumentation and procedures based on lessons learned during the implementation study, as well as a report on the implementation of a time-study and workload assessment at the local court level.

JUDICIAL LEADERSHIP

Strong judicial leadership is essential to successful implementation of reforms and improvements in how CPS and the courts process child maltreatment cases. Communities that have embraced ASFA and accomplished timely permanency for abused and neglected children have, without exception, benefited from judicial leadership. While judges alone cannot initiate change, their support and leadership are critical to reforming court practice.

Many communities across the country are fortunate to have judicial leaders in juvenile court who are committed to optimizing the ability of CPS and the courts to address effectively the needs of abused and neglected children and their families. Communities with model courts and strong State CIPs are good examples.

Like all effective leaders, judges must have a vision for what can and should be accomplished. For child abuse and neglect cases, that vision will include the timely achievement of safe, permanent homes for the children. The vision and how it is communicated by the words and actions of the judge and others who share it can motivate juvenile court practitioners and can provide meaning and value to their work. Areas in which judges' leadership can be exercised include court operations, interactions with other stakeholders, and advocacy for abused and neglected children.

Court Operations

Through the hearing and management of cases, judges set a standard for court operations, which includes the judges':

- Knowledge and skill in hearing, monitoring, and resolving individual cases;
- Commitment to timely proceedings and decisions;
- Enforcement of rules;
- Participation in training opportunities;
- Style of interacting with families and professionals.

This is important because good administrative leadership of court operations ensures that:

- The court has rules of procedure to guide practitioners;
- Petitions and other pleadings and documents are maintained in an orderly and accessible way;
- Cases are scheduled and decided on a timely basis, before the same judge, and at intervals that minimize waiting and inconvenience to participants;
- Continuances are rare;
- Decisions and orders are entered and distributed promptly.

Interactions with Other Stakeholders

Judicial leaders "...must encourage and promote collaboration and mutual respect among all participants in the child welfare system...," and "...should regularly convene representatives from [it] to improve operations of the system."[23] All effective juvenile courts are characterized by successful partnerships with CPS and with other community and system stakeholders. Judges meet regularly with these partners and work cooperatively with them to identify and resolve systemic problems, to plan training events, to strategize about new services to fulfi ll unmet needs, to address resource and funding issues, to improve service delivery and court processes, and to share their successes. These collaborative efforts create "...a synergy in which the contributions of the various partners enhance and magnify their individual effects."[24]

Advocacy for Abused and Neglected Children

Judicial leaders from the juvenile court should take an active role in educating policymakers and the public about the needs of child maltreatment victims. This includes new or expanded resources and services that are necessary to meet those needs, the importance of the work being done in the juvenile court, and the statutory changes necessary to enhance that work. Because of their position within the child welfare community, judges experienced in child maltreatment cases can be particularly effective in bringing about useful changes.

COURT MANAGEMENT INFORMATION SYSTEMS

Effective administrative leadership includes maintaining an information system that tracks individual and aggregate case data. For more information about the need for courts to have good management information systems for child abuse and neglect cases, as well as suggestions for improving existing capabilities and developing and implementing new systems, see:

- *Information Management: A Critical Component of Good Practice in Child Abuse and Neglect Cases;*
- *Model Court Approaches to Information Technology: A Dependency Court Data System Implementation Guide.*

CONCLUSION

Navigating the juvenile court process in child abuse and neglect cases can be an overwhelming experience for CPS caseworkers and the families they serve. However, a solid understanding of applicable child maltreatment legislation, various court proceedings, and court expectations will help CPS caseworkers enhance their case practice and outcomes. Furthermore, juvenile and family courts throughout the country are increasingly aware that innovative court practices and partnerships with CPS and community service providers are instrumental to achieving safety, permanency, and well-being for children and families.

End Notes

[1] U.S. Department of Health and Human Services, ACF. (2004) *General fi ndings from the Federal Child and Family Services Review* [On-line]. Available: *http://www.acf.hhs.gov/programs/cb/cwrp/results/* statefi ndings/genfi ndings04/genfi ndings04.pdf.

[2] Hardin, M. (2002a*). Child and Family Services Reviews (CFSRs): How judges, court administrators, and attorneys should be involved* [On-line]. Available: *http://www.abanet.org/child/courtimp.html.*

[3] Hardin, M. (2002b). *How and why to involve the courts in your Child and Family Services Review (CFSR): Suggestions for agency administrators* [Online]. Available: *http://www.abanet.org/child/* courtimp.html.

[4] Atwood, T. C., & Ravenel, V. R. (2005). Performance measures for courts: The next step in foster care reform. *Adoption Advocate* [On-line]. Available: *http://www.adoptioncouncil.org/documents/* Adoption_Advocate_ Vol_No_1_06_05.pdf.

[5] Fiermonte, C., & Sidote Salyers, N. (2005). *Improving outcomes together* [On-line]. Available: http:// jeritt.msu.edu/Documents/ABA_ Collaboration_Final_06-21 -05.pdf.

[6] Hardin, M. (2002b).

[7] Atwood, T. C., & Ravenel, V. R. (2005).

[8] Hardin, M. (2002a); National Child Welfare Resource Center on Legal and Judicial Issues. (2005). *Top ten ways legal professionals can help with CFSRs* [On-line]. Available: http://www.abanet.org/child/ courtimp.html.

[9] Hardin, M. (2002b).

[10] Hardin, M. (2002b).

[11] Pew Commission on Children in Foster Care. (2005). *About the Pew Commission on Children in Foster Care* [On-line]. Available: http://pewfostercare. org/about.

[12] Fiermonte, C., & Sidote Salyers, N. (2005).

[13] Fiermonte, C., & Sidote Salyers, N. (2005).

[14] Fiermonte, C., & Sidote Salyers, N. (2005).

[15] Fiermonte, C., & Sidote Salyers, N. (2005).

[16] U. S. Department of Health and Human Services, ACF. (2003). *Instructions for States applying for court improvement program funds for fi scal years 2003–2006* [On-line]. Available: http://www.acf.dhhs.gov/ programs/cb/laws/pi/pi0304.htm.

[17] U. S. Department of Health and Human Services, ACF. (2005). *Court involvement in the Child and Family Services Review* [On-line]. http://www.acf.hhs. gov/programs/cb/laws. pdf.

[18] The Social Security Act of 1935, 42 U.S.C. 629*h*; The Defi cit Reduction Act of 2005, Pub. L. No. 109-171, Title VII, Section 7401 (2005); The Social Security Act of 1935, 42 U.S.C. Title IV-E and Title IV-B; U.S. Department of Health and Human Services, ACF. (2006). *Instructions for state courts applying for new Court Improvement Program funds for fi scal years (FYs) 2006-2010* (ACYF-CB-PI-0605). Washington, DC: Author; Ohl, J. E. (2006). *Testimony on reauthorization of three Programs: The Mentoring of Children of Prisoners Program, the Promoting Safe and Stable Families Program, and the Court Improvement Program* [On-line]. Available: http://www.hhs.gov/asl/ testify/t0605 1 0.html.

[19] Mentaberry, M. (1999, January). Model courts serve abused and neglected children. *OJJDP Fact Sheet.* Washington, DC: U.S. Department of Justice, OJP, Office of Juvenile Justice and Delinquency Prevention (OJJDP).

[20] Goldsmith, D. J. (2002). In the best interest of an Indian child: The Indian Child Welfare Act. *Juvenile and Family Court Journal, 53*(4), 9–17.

[31] Feller, J. N., Davidson, H. A., Hardin, M., & Horowitz, R. M. (1992). *Working With the courts in child protection* [On-line]. Available: http://www. childwelfare.gov/pubs/ usermanuals/ courts/index.cfm.

[22] U. S. Department of Justice, OJP, OJJDP. (2003). *Notice of solicitation for the Strengthening Abuse and Neglect Courts in America: Management Information Systems Project, 68 Fed. Reg. 14699–14705* [On-line]. Available: http://www.ojp.usdoj.gov/docs/SANCA. txt.

[23] National Council of Juvenile and Family Court Judges. (1999, October). Key principles for permanency planning for children. *Technical Assistance Brief* [On-line]. Available: http:// www.ncjfcj.org/images/stories/dept/ppcd/ pdf/ tabriefkeyprinciples.pdf.

[24] Rottman, D. B., Casey, P., & Efkeman, H. (1998, February). *Court and community collaboration: Ends and means: A discussion paper* [On-line]. Available: *http://www.courtinfo.ca.gov/programs/community/* endsmeansfoot.htm.

APPENDIX A - GLOSSARY OF TERMS

Adjournment – the suspension of business or sessions, either for a fixed time, indefinitely, or until the opening of another term.

Adjudicatory Hearings – held by the juvenile and family court to determine whether a child has been maltreated or whether another legal basis exists for the State to intervene to protect the child.

Adoption and Safe Families Act (ASFA) – signed into law November 1997 and designed to improve the safety of children, to promote adoption and other permanent homes for children who need them, and to support families. The law requires CPS agencies to provide more timely and focused assessment and intervention services to the children and families that are served within the CPS system.

CASA – court-appointed special advocates (usually volunteers) who serve to ensure that the needs and interests of a child in child protection judicial proceedings are fully protected.

Case Closure – the process of ending the relationship between the CPS worker and the family that often involves a mutual assessment of progress. Optimally, cases are closed when families have achieved their goals and the risk of maltreatment has been reduced or eliminated.

Case Plan – the casework document that outlines the outcomes, goals, and tasks necessary to be achieved in order to reduce the risk of maltreatment.

Case Planning – the stage of the CPS case process where the CPS caseworker develops a case plan with the family members.

Caseworker Competency – demonstrated professional behaviors based on the knowledge, skills, personal qualities, and values a person holds.

Central Registry – a centralized database containing information on all substantiated/founded reports of child maltreatment in a selected area (typically a State).

Child Abuse Prevention and Treatment Act (CAPTA) – see Keeping Children and Families Safe Act.

Child Protective Services (CPS) – the designated social services agency (in most States) to receive reports, investigate, and provide intervention and treatment services to children and families in which child maltreatment has occurred. Frequently, this agency is located within larger public social service agencies, such as Departments of Social Services.

Civil Contempt – the willful failure to do something that a court has ordered, such as refusing to testify when the court has found that no privilege applies or refusing to pay child support when there are ample funds to do so. The usual sanction is incarceration for a term that lasts until the person in contempt complies with the court order.

Concurrent Planning – identifies alternative plans for permanent placement of a child by addressing both reunification and legal permanency with a new parent or caregiver if reunification efforts fail.

Consent Decree – a decree entered by a court that is determined by the parties' agreement; a settlement between the parties that is subject to judicial approval and supervision.

Continuance – an adjournment of a case from one day to another or to a later hour of the same day.

Criminal Contempt – an act that obstructs justice or attacks the integrity of the court that is punishable by fine or imprisonment or both. Criminal contempt may be indirect or direct. Indirect contempt is contempt occurring outside the courtroom, such as a willful violation of a court's order. Direct contempt is disruptive or disrespectful behavior that occurs in the presence of the judge, such as uttering an epithet when the judge announces an unfavorable decision.

Cross-examination – questioning of a witness by attorneys other than the one who called the person as a witness.

Cultural Competence – a set of attitudes, behaviors, and policies that integrates knowledge about groups of people into practices and standards to enhance the quality of services to all cultural groups being served.

Declaratory Judgment – a court decision which simply declares the rights of the parties or expresses the opinion of the court on a question of law without ordering anything to be done.

Delinquency – the commitment of an offense by a youth of what would be a crime if he or she were an adult.

Dependent Child – as used in statues providing for the care of dependent, neglected, and delinquent children, the term means dependent upon the public support; any child under the age of 18 who is destitute, or whose home by reason of neglect by the parents is an unfit place for such child, or whose father, mother, guardian, or custodian does not properly provide for such a child.

Differential Response – an area of CPS reform that offers greater flexibility in responding to allegations of abuse and neglect. Also referred to as "dual track" or "multi-track" response, it permits CPS agencies to respond differentially to children's needs for safety, the degree of risk present, and the family's needs for services and support. See "dual track."

Discovery – pretrial process that allows each party to obtain information relevant to the case from the other parties.

Depositions – transcribed oral examinations under oath.

Dispositional Hearings – held by the juvenile and family court to determine the legal resolution of cases after adjudication, such as whether placement of the child in out-of-home care is necessary, and what services the children and family will need to reduce the risk and to address the effects of maltreatment.

Dual Track – term reflecting new CPS response systems that typically combine a non adversarial service-based assessment track for cases where children are not at immediate risk with a traditional CPS investigative track for cases where children are unsafe or at greater risk for maltreatment. See "differential response."

Duces Tecum – a type of subpoena or court order that requires a person to produce for the court specified documents or records.

Due Process – The principle that every person has the protection of a day in court, representation by an attorney, and the benefit of procedures that are speedy, fair, and impartial.

Evaluation of Family Progress – the stage of the CPS case process where the CPS caseworker measures changes in family behaviors and conditions (risk factors), monitors risk elimination or reduction, assesses strengths, and determines case closure.

Exculpatory – evidence or testimony that exonerates or clears the defendant.

Ex Parte – on behalf of or involving only one party to a legal matter and in the absence of and usually without notice to the other party.

Expert Testimony – opinion testimony about a subject that is outside the judge's or jury's knowledge or experience, provided by a witness with established expertise on that subject.

Family Assessment – the stage of the child protection process when the CPS caseworker, community treatment provider, and the family reach a mutual understanding regarding the behaviors and conditions that must change to reduce or eliminate the risk of maltreatment, the most critical treatment needs that must be addressed, and the strengths on which to build.

Family Drug Court – a drug court that deals with cases involving parental rights in which an adult is the litigant (i.e., any party to a lawsuit, which means plaintiff, defendant, petitioner, respondent, cross- complainant and cross-defendant, but not a witness or attorney); the case comes before the court through either a criminal or civil proceeding; and the case arises out of the substance abuse of a parent.

Family Group Conferencing – a family meeting model used by CPS agencies to optimize family strengths in the planning process. This model brings the family, extended family, and others important in the family's life (e.g., friends, clergy, neighbors) together to make decisions regarding how best to ensure safety of the family members.

Family Unity Model – a family meeting model used by CPS agencies to optimize family strengths in the planning process. This model is similar to the Family Group Conferencing model.

Full Disclosure – information provided to the family regarding the steps in the CPS intervention process, the requirements of CPS, the expectations of the family, the consequences if the family does not fulfill the expectations, and the rights of the parents to ensure that the family completely understands the process.

Guardian ad Litem – a lawyer or layperson who represents a child in juvenile or family court. Usually this person considers the "best interest" of the child and may perform a variety of roles, including those of independent investigator, advocate, advisor, and guardian for the child. A layperson who serves in this role is sometimes known as a court-appointed special advocate or CASA.

Hearsay – an out-of-court statement made by someone other than the witness that is offered for the truth of that statement.

Home Visitation Programs – prevention programs that offer a variety of family-focused services to pregnant mothers and families with new babies. Activities frequently encompass structured visits to the family's home and may address positive parenting practices, nonviolent discipline techniques, child development, maternal and child health, available services, and advocacy.

Immunity – established in all child abuse laws to protect reporters from civil law suits and criminal prosecution resulting from filing a report of child abuse and neglect.

Initial Assessment or Investigation – the stage of the CPS case process where the CPS caseworker determines the validity of the child maltreatment report, assesses the risk of maltreatment, determines if the child is safe, develops a safety plan if needed to assure the child's protection, and determines services needed.

Injunction – an equitable remedy in the form of a court order compelling a party to do or refrain from doing a specified act.

Intake – the stage of the CPS case process where the CPS caseworker screens and accepts reports of child maltreatment.

Interview Protocol – a structured format to ensure that all family members are seen in a planned strategy, that community providers collaborate, and that information gathering is thorough.

Jurisdiction – the power or right to exercise authority.

Juvenile and Family Courts – established in most States to resolve conflict and to otherwise intervene in the lives of families in a manner that promotes the best interest of children. These courts specialize in areas such as child maltreatment, domestic violence, juvenile delinquency, divorce, child custody, and child support.

Juvenile Drug Court – a drug court that focuses on juvenile delinquency matters and status offenses that involve juveniles who are substance abusers.

Keeping Children and Families Safe Act – The Keeping Children and Families Safe Act of 2003 (P.L. 108–36) included the reauthorization of the Child Abuse Prevention and Treatment Act (CAPTA) in its Title I, Sec. 111. CAPTA provides minimum standards for defining child physical abuse and neglect and sexual abuse that States must incorporate into their statutory definitions in order to receive Federal funds. CAPTA defines child abuse and neglect as "at a minimum, any recent act or failure to act on the part of a parent or caretaker, which results in death, serious physical or emotional harm, sexual abuse or exploitation, or an act or failure to act which presents an imminent risk of serious harm."

Kinship Care – formal child placement by the juvenile court and child welfare agency in the home of a child's relative.

Liaison – the designation of a person within an organization who has responsibility for facilitating communication, collaboration, and coordination between agencies involved in the child protection system.

Litigant – a party to a lawsuit.

Mandated Reporter – individuals required by State statutes to report suspected child abuse and neglect to the proper authorities (usually CPS or law enforcement agencies). Mandated reporters typically include professionals, such as educators and other school personnel, health care and mental health professionals, social workers, childcare providers, and law enforcement officers. Some States identify all citizens as mandated reporters.

Multidisciplinary Team – established between agencies and professionals within the child protection system to discuss cases of child abuse and neglect and to aid in decisions at various stages of the CPS case process. These teams also may be designated by different names, including child protection teams, interdisciplinary teams, or case consultation teams.

Neglect – the failure to provide for a child's basic needs. Neglect can be physical, educational, or emotional. *Physical neglect* can include not providing adequate food or clothing, appropriate medical care, supervision, or proper weather protection (heat or coats). *Educational neglect* includes failure to provide appropriate schooling, special educational needs, or allowing excessive truancies. *Psychological neglect* includes the lack of any emotional support and love, chronic inattention to the child, exposure to spouse abuse, or drug and alcohol abuse.

Out-of-Home Care – childcare, foster care, or residential care provided by persons, organizations, and institutions to children who are placed outside their families, usually under the jurisdiction of juvenile or family court.

Overrule – to set aside the authority of a former decision; the act of court in rejecting a motion or objection made by a party to a lawsuit.

***Parens Patriae* Doctrine** – originating in feudal England, a doctrine that vests in the State a right of guardianship of minors. This concept has gradually evolved into the principle that the community, in addition to the parent, has a strong interest in the care and nurturing of children. Schools, juvenile courts, and social service agencies all derive their authority from the State's power to protect children who are unable to protect themselves.

Parent or Caretaker – person responsible for the care of the child.

Petitions – a document containing allegations of child abuse or neglect that is typically filed by the CPS attorney in juvenile court.

Physical Abuse – the inflicting of a non-accidental physical injury upon a child. This may include, burning, hitting, punching, shaking, kicking, beating, or otherwise harming a child. It may, however, have been the result of over-discipline or physical punishment that is inappropriate to the child's age.

Preponderance of the Evidence – the burden of proof for civil cases in most States, including child maltreatment proceedings. The attorney for CPS or other petitioner must show by a preponderance of evidence that the abuse or neglect happened. This standard means that the evidence is more credible than the evidence presented by the defendant party.

Primary Prevention – activities geared to a sample of the general population to prevent child abuse and neglect from occurring. Also referred to as "universal prevention."

Protective Factors – strengths and resources that appear to mediate or serve as a "buffer" against risk factors that contribute to vulnerability to maltreatment or against the negative effects of maltreatment experiences.

Protocol – an interagency agreement that delineates joint roles and responsibilities by establishing criteria and procedures for working together on cases of child abuse and neglect.

Psychological Maltreatment – a pattern of caregiver behavior or extreme incidents that convey to children that they are worthless, fl awed, unloved, unwanted, endangered, or only of value to meeting another's needs. This can include parents or caretakers using extreme or bizarre forms of punishment or threatening or terrorizing a child. The term "psychological maltreatment" is also known as emotional abuse or neglect, verbal abuse, or mental abuse.

Putative Father – the alleged or supposed male parent; the person alleged to have fathered a child whose parentage is at issue.

Respondent – an answering party in a proceeding in juvenile or family court.

Response Time – a determination made by CPS and law enforcement regarding the immediacy of the response needed to a report of child abuse or neglect.

Review Hearings – held by the juvenile and family court to review dispositions (usually every 6 months) and to determine the need to maintain placement in out-of-home care or court jurisdiction of a child.

Risk – the likelihood that a child will be maltreated in the future.

Risk Assessment – to assess and measure the likelihood that a child will be maltreated in the future, frequently through the use of checklists, matrices, scales, and other methods of measurement.

Risk Factors – behaviors and conditions present in the child, parent, or family that likely will contribute to child maltreatment occurring in the future.

Safety – absence of an imminent or immediate threat of moderate-to-serious harm to the child.

Safety Assessment – a part of the CPS case process in which available information is analyzed to identify whether a child is in immediate danger of moderate or serious harm.

Safety Plan – a casework document developed when it is determined that the child is in imminent or potential risk of serious harm. In the safety plan, the caseworker targets the factors that are causing or contributing to the risk of imminent serious harm to the child, and identifies, along with the family, the interventions that will control the safety factors and ensure the child's protection.

Secondary Prevention – activities targeted to prevent breakdowns and dysfunctions among families who have been identified as at risk for abuse and neglect.

Service or Constructive Service – the act of delivering to, or informing someone of, a writ, summons, or other notice as prescribed by law.

Service Agreement – the casework document developed between the CPS caseworker and the family that outlines the tasks necessary to achieve goals and outcomes necessary for risk reduction.

Service Provision – the stage of the CPS casework process when CPS and other service providers deliver specific services geared toward the reduction of risk of maltreatment.

Sexual Abuse – inappropriate adolescent or adult sexual behavior with a child. It includes fondling a child's genitals, making the child fondle the adult's genitals, intercourse, incest, rape, sodomy, exhibitionism, sexual exploitation, or exposure to pornography. To be considered child abuse, these acts have to be committed by a person responsible for the care of a child (for example a baby-sitter, a parent, or a daycare provider) or related to the child. If a stranger commits these acts, it would be considered sexual assault and handled solely by the police and criminal courts.

Status Offender – a juvenile under the jurisdiction of the court because of acts that would not be criminal if committed by an adult, but that indicate that the child is beyond parental control.

Status Offenses – transgressions of children that would not be crimes if they were legal age; primarily involve running away and truancy. The age for bringing such charges varies from State to State.

Substantiated – an investigation disposition concluding that the allegation of maltreatment or risk of maltreatment was supported or founded, as defined by State law or State policy. A CPS determination means that credible evidence exists that child abuse or neglect has occurred.

Suspended Sentence – a sentence that the defendant will not have to serve if he or she complies with the conditions of probation.

Sustain – to allow or uphold as valid.

Termination of Parental Rights Hearing – a legal proceeding to free a child from a parent's legal custody so that others can adopt the child. The legal basis for termination of parental rights differs from State to State, but most States consider the failure of the parent to support or communicate with the child for a specified period, parental failure to improve home conditions, extreme or repeated neglect or abuse, parental incapacity to care for the child, and/or extreme deterioration of the parent-child relationship. In making this finding, the court is determining that the parents will not be able to provide adequate care for the child in the future by using a standard of clear and convincing evidence. This burden of proof is higher than preponderance of the evidence, which is used in civil abuse or neglect cases where termination is not sought.

Tertiary Prevention – treatment efforts geared to address situations where child maltreatment has already occurred, with the goals of preventing child maltreatment from occurring in the future and of avoiding the harmful effects of child maltreatment.

Transactional Immunity – a broader form of use immunity that bars prosecution of a witness for any event or transaction described in the witness's compelled testimony, regardless of the source of the evidence against that person.

Treatment – the stage of the child protection case process when specific services are provided by CPS and other providers to reduce the risk of maltreatment, support families in meeting case goals, and address the effects of maltreatment.

Universal Prevention – activities and services directed at the general public with the goal of stopping the occurrence of maltreatment before it starts. Also referred to as "primary prevention."

Unsubstantiated (not substantiated) – an investigation disposition that determines that there is not sufficient evidence under State law or policy to conclude that the child has been maltreated or is at risk of maltreatment. A CPS determination means that credible evidence does not exist that child abuse or neglect has occurred.

Use Immunity – bars the use of a witness's compelled testimony and statements from being used directly or indirectly against that person in a subsequent trial.

Voir Dire – the inquiry of prospective jurors to determine if the jurors are fit for jury duty in a given case.

APPENDIX B - RESOURCE LISTINGS OF SELECTED NATIONAL ORGANIZATIONS CONCERNED WITH CHILD MALTREATMENT

Listed below are several of the many national organizations and groups dealing with various aspects of child maltreatment. Visit http://childwelfare.gov/pubs/usermanual.cfm to view a more comprehensive list of resources and visit http://www. childwelfare.gov/ organizations/index.cfm to view an organization database. Inclusion on this list is for information purposes only and does not constitute an endorsement by the Office on Child Abuse and Neglect or the Children's Bureau.

CHILD WELFARE ORGANIZATIONS

American Humane Association Children's Division

address: 63 Inverness Dr., East
Englewood, CO 80112-5117
phone: (800) 227-4645
(303) 792-9900
fax: (303) 792-5333
e-mail: children
Web site: http://www.americanhumane.org

Conducts research, analysis, and training to help public and private agencies respond to child maltreatment.

American Professional Society on the Abuse of Children

address: P.O. Box 30669
Charleston, SC 29417
phone: (843) 764-2905
877) 40A-PSAC
fax: (803) 753-9823
e-mail: tricia-williams@ouhsc.edu
Web site: www.apsac.org

Provides professional education, promotes research to inform effective practice, and addresses public policy issues. Professional membership organization.

American Public Human Services Association

address: 810 First St., NE, Suite 500
Washington, DC 20002-4267
phone: (202) 682-0100
fax: (202) 289-6555
Web site: http://www.aphsa.org

Addresses program and policy issues related to the administration and delivery of publicly funded human services. Professional membership organization.

AVANCE Family Support and Education Program

address: 118 N. Medina
San Antonio, TX 78207
phone: (210) 270-4630
fax: (210) 270-4612
Web site: www.avance.org

Operates a national training center to share and disseminate information, material, and curricula to service providers and policy-makers interested in supporting high-risk Hispanic families.

Child Welfare League of America

address: 440 First St., NW, Third Floor
Washington, DC 20001-2085
phone: (202) 638-2952
fax: (202) 638-4004
Web site: http://www.cwla.org

Provides training, consultation, and technical assistance to child welfare professionals and agencies while also educating the public about emerging issues affecting children.

National Association of Counsel for Children

Address: 1825 Marion Street, Suite 242
Denver, CO 80218
phone: (888) 828-NACC
e-mail: advocate@NACCchildlaw.org
Web site: http://www.naccchildlaw.org

Provides training and technical assistance to child advocates and works to improve the child welfare, juvenile justice and private custody systems.

National Black Child Development Institute

address: 1101 15th St., NW, Suite 900
Washington, DC 20005
phone: (202) 833-2220
fax: (202) 833-8222
e-mail: moreinfo@nbcdi.org
Web site: www.nbcdi.org

Operates programs and sponsors a national training conference through Howard University to improve and protect the well-being of African-American children.

National Center for State Courts

address: 300 Newport Ave.
Williamsburg, VA 23185-4147
phone: (800) 616-6164
fax: (757) 564-2022
Web site: http://www.ncsconline.org

Enhances court operations with the latest technology, collects and interprets the latest data on court operations nationwide, and provides information on proven "best practices" for improving court operations.

National Children's Advocacy Center

address: 210 Pratt Ave
Huntsville AL 35801
phone: (256) 533-KIDS
fax: (256) 534-6883
Web site: http://www.nationalcac.org

Provides prevention, intervention, and treatment services to physically and sexually abused children and their families within a child-focused team approach.

National Council of Juvenile and Family Court Judges

address: NCJFCJ – Permanency Planning for Children Department
1041 North Virginia St.
P.O. Box 8970
Reno, NV 89507
phone: (775) 784-6012
fax: (775) 784-6628
email: admin@ncjfcj.org
Web site: http://www.pppncjfcj.org

Serves the Nation's children and families by improving the courts of juvenile and family jurisdictions. Its mission is to better the justice system through education and applied research and improve the standards, practices, and effectiveness of the juvenile court system. NCJFCJ strives to increase awareness and sensitivity to children's issues and focuses on providing meaningful assistance to the judges, court administrators, and related professionals in whose care the concerns of children and their families have been entrusted.

National Court Appointed Special Advocate Association

address: North Tower, 100 West Harrison St.,
Suite 500
Seattle, WA 98119-4123
phone: (800) 628-3233
fax: (206) 270-0078
email: inquiry@nationalcasa.org
Web site: http://www.nationalcasa.org

Promotes and supports volunteer advocacy in juvenile courts for children alleged to be maltreated. It receives Federal and private funding, provides money and technical assistance to start and expand programs, promulgates performance standards, produces training reports and other publications, and trains program leaders and volunteers.

National Indian Child Welfare Association

address: 5100 SW Macadam Ave.,
Suite 300
Portland, OR 97239
phone: (503) 222-4044
fax: (503) 222-4007
e-mail: info@nicwa.org
Web site: http://www.nicwa.org

Disseminates information and provides technical assistance on Indian child welfare issues. Supports community development and advocacy efforts to facilitate tribal responses to the needs of families and children.

Youth Law Center

address: Children's Legal Protection Center
1010 Vermont Ave., NW, Suite 310
Washington, DC 20005-4902
phone: (202) 637-0377
fax: (202) 379-1600
e-mail: info@youthlawcenter.com
Web site: http://www.youthlawcenter.com

Works to ensure that vulnerable children are provided with the conditions and services they need, particularly focusing on children living apart from their families in child welfare and juvenile justice systems.

NATIONAL RESOURCE CENTERS

National Child Welfare Resource Center on Legal and Judicial Issues

address: ABA Center on Children and the Law
740 15th St., NW
Washington, DC 20005-1019
phone: (800) 285-2221 (Service Center)
(202) 662-1720
fax: (202) 662-1755
e-mail: ctrchildlaw@abanet.org
Web site: http://www.abanet.org/child/rclji/home. html

Provides technical assistance, training and consultation to State, local and Tribal agencies and courts to strengthen their knowledge of legal and judicial issues related to child welfare and juvenile and family courts. Its expertise on a wide variety of subjects includes court improvement, agency and court collaboration, termination of parental rights, non-adversarial case resolution, reasonable efforts requirements, legal representation of children, permanent guardianship, confidentiality, and other emerging child welfare issues.

National Resource Center for Adoption

address: 16250 Northland Drive, Suite 120
Southfi eld, MI 48075
phone: (248) 443-0306
fax: (248) 443-7099
e-mail: nrc@nrcadoption.org
Web site: http://www.nrcadoption.org

Develops and distributes training curricula, publications, and videos and sponsors three national conferences to improve the effectiveness and quality of adoption and post-adoption services. The center also provides training on current practices, policies, and issues in special needs adoption; permanency planning; post-adoption services; and cultural competence.

National Resource Center for Child Protective Services

address: 925 #4 Sixth Street NW
Albuquerque, New Mexico 87102
phone: (505) 345-2444
fax: (505) 345-2626
e-mail: theresa.costello@actionchildprotection.org
Web site: http://www.nrccps.org

Focuses on building State, local, and Tribal capacity through training and technical assistance in CPS, includingmeeting Federal requirements, strengthening programs, eligibility for the CAPTA grant, support to State Liaison Officers, and collaboration with other NRCs.

National Resource Center on Domestic Violence: Child Protection and Custody

address: Family Violence Department National Council of Juvenile and Family Court Judges
P.O. Box 8970
Reno, NV 89507
phone: (800) 527-3223
fax: (775) 784-6160

e-mail: fvdinfo@ncjfcj.org
Web site: http://www.ncjfcj.org/dept/fvd/res_center

Promotes improved court responses to family violence through demonstration programs, professional training, technical assistance, national conferences, and publications.

National Resource Center for Family-Centered Practice and Permanency Planning

address: National Resource Center for Family- Centered Practice and Permanency Planning
Hunter College School of Social Work
129 East 79th Street
New York, NY 10021
phone: (212) 452-7053
fax: (212) 452-7475
Web site: http://www.hunter.cuny.edu/socwork/ nrcfcpp/

Provides training and technical assistance and information services to help States through all stages of the CFSRs, emphasizing family-centered principles and practices and helping States build knowledge of foster care issues. Partners with the Child Welfare League of America and the National Indian Child Welfare Association to provide training, technical assistance, and information services.

Technical Assistance Support System Organizations

Interstate Compact on Adoption and Medical Assistance

address: Association of Administrators of the Interstate Compact on Adoption and Medical Assistance
810 First St., NE, Suite 500
Washington, DC 20002
phone: (202) 682-0100
fax: (202) 289-6555
Web site: http://aaicama.aphsa.org/index.html

Provides technical and legal assistance, education and training, and materials on practice and policy issues to facilitate the administration of the Interstate Compact on Adoption and Medical Assistance.

Interstate Compact on the Placement of Children

address: Association of Administrators of the Interstate Compact on the Placement of Children
American Public Human Services Association
810 First St., NE, Suite 500
Washington, DC 20002-4267
phone: (202) 682-0100
fax: (202) 289-6555
e-mail: ICPCinbox@aphsa.org
Web site: http://icpc.aphsa.org

Provides ongoing administrative, legal, and technical assistance to individual States that administer the Interstate Compact on the Placement of Children, which is a uniform State law that establishes a contract among party States to ensure that children placed across State lines receive adequate protection and services.

PREVENTION ORGANIZATIONS

National Alliance of Children's Trust and Prevention Funds

address: 5712 30th Ave. NE
Seattle, WA 98105
phone: 206-526-1221
fax: 206-526-0220
e-mail: trafael@juno.com
Web site: www.ctfalliance.org

Assists State children's trust and prevention funds to strengthen families and protect children from harm.

Prevent Child Abuse America

address: 200 South Michigan Ave.,
17th Floor
Chicago, IL 60604-2404
phone: (800) 835-2671 (orders)
(312) 663-3520
fax: (312) 939-8962
e-mail: mailbox@preventchildabuse.org
Web site: http://www.preventchildabuse.org

Conducts prevention activities such as public awareness campaigns, advocacy, networking, research, and publishing, and provides information and statistics on child abuse.

Shaken Baby Syndrome Prevention Plus

address: 649 Main St., Suite B
Groveport, OH 43125
phone: (800) 858-5222
(614) 836-8360
fax: (614) 836-8359
e-mail: sbspp@aol.com
Web site: http://www.sbsplus.com

Develops, studies, and disseminates information and materials designed to prevent shaken baby syndrome and other forms of child abuse and to increase positive parenting and child care.

COMMUNITY PARTNERS

The Center for Faith-Based and Community Initiatives

address: U. S. Department of Health and Human Services
200 Independence Ave., SW.
Washington, DC 20201
phone: 1-877-696-6775
e-mail: cfbci@hhs.gov

Web site: http://www.hhs.gov/faith

Welcomes the participation of faith-based and community-based organizations as valued and essential partners with the U.S. Department of Health and Human Services. Funding goes to faith- based organizations through Head Start, programs for refugee resettlement, runaway and homeless youth, independent living, childcare, child support enforcement, and child welfare.

Family Support America
(formerly Family Resource Coalition of America)

address: 205 West Randolph Street,
Suite 2222
Chicago, IL 60606
phone: (312) 338-0900
fax: (312) 338-1522
e-mail: info@familysupportamerica.org
Web site: www.familysupportamerica.org

Works to strengthen and empower families and communities so that they can foster the optimal development of children, youth, and adult family members.

National Exchange Club Foundation for the Prevention of Child Abuse

address: 3050 Central Ave.
Toledo, OH 43606-1700
phone: (800) 924-2643
(419) 535-3232
fax: (419) 535-1989
e-mail: info@preventchildabuse.com
Web site: http://www.nationalexchangeclub.com

Conducts local campaigns in the fi ght against child abuse by providing education, intervention, and support to families affected by child maltreatment.

National Fatherhood Initiative

address: 101 Lake Forest Blvd., Suite 360
Gaithersburg, MD 20877
phone: (301) 948-0599
fax: (301) 948-4325
Web site: http://www.fatherhood

Works to improve the well-being of children by increasing the proportion of children growing up with involved, responsible, and committed fathers.

FOR THE GENERAL PUBLIC

Childhelp USA

address: 15757 North 78th St.
Scottsdale, AZ 85260
phone: (800) 4-A-CHILD
(800) 2-A-CHILD (TDD line)
(480) 922-8212
fax: (480) 922-7061
e-mail: help@childhelpusa.org
Web site: http://www.childhelpusa.org

Provides crisis counseling to adult survivors and child victims of child abuse, off enders, and parents, and operates a national hotline.

National Center for Missing and Exploited Children

address: Charles B. Wang International Children's Building
699 Prince St.
Alexandria, VA 22314-3175
phone: (800) 843-5678
(703) 274-3900
fax: (703) 274-2220
Web site: http://www.missingkids.com

Provides assistance to parents, children, law enforcement, schools, and the community in recovering missing children and raising public awareness about ways to help prevent child abduction, molestation, and sexual exploitation.

Parents Anonymous

address: 675 West Foothill Blvd., Suite 220
Claremont, CA 91711
phone: (909) 621-6184
fax: (909) 625-6304
e-mail: Parentsanonymous@parentsanonymous.org
Web site: www.parentsanonymous.org

Leads mutual support groups to help parents provide nurturing environments for their families.

For More Information

Child Welfare Information Gateway

address: 1250 Maryland Avenue, SW
Eighth Floor
Washington, DC 20024
phone: (800) 394-3366
(703) 385-7565
fax: (703) 385-3206
e-mail: info@childwelfare.gov
Web site: http://www.childwelfare.gov/

Collects, stores, catalogs, and disseminates information on all aspects of child maltreatment, child welfare, and adoption to help build the capacity of professionals in the fi eld. A service of the Children's Bureau.

APPENDIX C- STATE TELEPHONE NUMBERS FOR REPORTING CHILD ABUSE

Each State designates specific agencies to receive and investigate reports of suspected child abuse and neglect. Typically, this responsibility is carried out by child protective services (CPS) within a Department of Social Services, Department of Human Resources, or Division of Family and Children Services. In some States, police departments also may receive reports of child abuse or neglect.

Many States have local or toll-free telephone numbers, listed below, for reporting suspected abuse. The reporting party must be calling from the same State where the child is allegedly being abused for most of the following numbers to be valid.

For States not listed, or when the reporting party resides in a different State from the child, please call Childhelp, 800-4-A-Child (800-422-4453), or your local CPS agency. States may occasionally change the telephone numbers listed below. To view the most current contact information, including State Web addresses, visit http://www.childwelfare.gov/pubs/reslist/rl_dsp.cfm?rs_id=5&rate_chno=11-11172.

Alabama (AL)
334-242-9500

Alaska (AK)
800-478-4444

Arizona (AZ)
888-SOS-CHILD
(888-767-2445)

Indiana (IN)
800-800-5556

Iowa (IA)
800-362-2178

Kansas (KS)
800-922-5330

Kentucky (KY)

New Hampshire (NH)
800-894-5533
603-271-6556

New Jersey (NJ)
877-652-2873
800-835-5510(TDD/TTY))

Arkansas (AR)
800-482-5964

Colorado (CO)
303-866-5932

Connecticut (CT)
800-842-2288
800-624-5518 (TDD)

Delaware (DE)
800-292-9582

District of Columbia (DC)
202-671-SAFE (7233)

Florida (FL)
800-96-ABUSE
(800-962-2873)

Hawaii (HI)
808-832-5300

Idaho (ID)
800-926-2588

Illinois (IL)
800-252-2873
217-524-2606

800-752-6200

Maine (ME)
800-452-1999
800-963-9490
(TTY)

Massachusetts (MA)
800-792-5200

Mississippi (MS)
800-222-8000
601-359-4991

Missouri (MO)
800-392-3738
573-751-3448

Montana (MT)
866-820-KIDS
(5437)

Nebraska (NE)
800-652-1999

Nevada (NV)
800-992-5757
775-684-4400

New Mexico (NM)
800-797-3260
505-841-6100

New York (NY)
800-342-3720
518-474-8740
800-369-2437
(TDD)

Oklahoma (OK)
800-522-3511

Pennsylvania (PA)
800-932-0313

Puerto Rico (PR)
800-981-8333
787-749-1333

Rhode Island (RI)
800-RI-CHILD
(800-742-4453)

South Carolina (SC)
803-898-7318

South Dakota (SD)
605-773-3227

Tennessee (TN)
877-237-0004

Texas (TX)
800-252-5400
512-834-3784

Utah (UT)
800-678-9399

Vermont (VT)
800-649-5285
(after hours)

Virginia (VA)
800-552-7096
804-786-8536

Washington (WA)
866-END-HARM
(866-363-4276)
800-562-5624
(after hours)
800-624-6186
(TTY)

West Virginia (WV)
800-352-6513

Appendix D - Guidelines for Child Protection Services Caseworkers for Permanency and Review Hearings

Individuals Who Should Be Present at Both Permanency and Review Hearings

- The judge who has monitored the case from the first hearing;
- The child, unless inappropriate for a specific reason;
- The parent whose rights have not been relinquished or terminated;
- The attorney for the parent;
- The assigned social services caseworker;
- The prosecuting or agency attorney;
- For Indian children, a representative from the child's tribe and tribal attorney, if any;
- The guardian ad litem for the child, whether attorney, social worker, or other paid nonattorney, volunteer, or Court-Appointed Special Advocate;
- The attorney for the child, if applicable;
- The foster parent, legal-risk foster parent, or adoptive parent;
- Relatives, other interested persons, and witnesses;
- The court reporter or suitable recording technology;
- The court security and other court staff .

Questions for All Cases: What Are the Child's Special Needs?

- What is the child's health and education status?
- What is being offered to address the child's cultural needs, if applicable?
- What is the child's current placement adjustment?
- What services are being provided to the child, what progress has the child made, and what issues still need to be addressed?

For the Permanency Hearing

If Reunification Is Recommended:

- How have the conditions or circumstances leading to the removal of the child been corrected?
- Why is this plan in the best interests of the child?
- How often is visitation occurring and what is the impact on the child?
- What is the date and detailed plan for the child's safe return home and follow-up supervision after family reunification?
- What are the plans to continue any necessary services to the child?
- What are the plans to continue any necessary services to the family?
- If a change of school will occur, what will be done to prepare for the transition?

If Termination of Parental Rights and Adoption Are Recommended:

- What are the facts and circumstances supporting the grounds for termination?
- What reasonable efforts were made to reunify?
- Why is this plan in the best interests of the child?
- Has the petition been filed and, if not, what is the date it will be filed?
- Are there relatives who will adopt the child if termination of parental rights is granted? If so, is the child living with the relative? If not, why not? If there are no relatives willing and able to adopt, why not?

- If relative adoption is not the plan, is adoption by the foster parents the plan? If not, why not?
- If an adoptive home must be recruited, what efforts are being made to identify potential adoptive homes both locally and in other jurisdictions? Are there adults with whom the child has a positive relationship and are they potential adopting families?

Will Adoption With Contact Be Recommended and Why or Why Not?

- What counseling will occur to assist the child to deal with this change of plan?
- If the child is an Indian child, have Indian Child Welfare Act requirements been met?

If Permanent Guardianship or Permanent Custody is Recommended:

- Why is this option preferable to termination of parental rights and adoption? Why is it in the best interests of the child?
- What reasonable efforts were made to reunify?
- What are the facts and circumstances demonstrating the appropriateness of the individual or couple to serve as permanent family to the child? Is there another person who spends significant time in the home, and if so, has that individual been interviewed for appropriateness?
- Has there been full disclosure to the family of the child's circumstances and special needs?
- What is the plan to ensure that this will be a permanent home for the child?
- What contact will occur between the child and parents, siblings, and other family members?
- What financial support will be provided by the biological parents?
- What are the plans to continue any necessary services to the child? How will these services be funded after guardianship or custody has been granted?
- If the child is not already placed in this home, why not and:
    - How often is visitation occurring and what is the impact on the child?

- What is the date and detailed plan for the child's placement in this home and follow-up supervision after placement?
- If a change of school will occur, what will be done to prepare for the transition?

If Another Plan Is Being Recommended:

- What are the compelling reasons not to proceed with reunification, termination of parental rights, permanent guardianship, or permanent custody? What is the plan, and why is this plan in the child's best interests?
- What reasonable efforts were made to reunify the child with the parent?
- How will this plan provide stability and permanency for the child?
- What contact will occur between child and parents, siblings, and other family members?
- What are the plans to continue any necessary services to the child?
- If the child is a teenager, what is the plan to prepare the child for independent living?
- If the child is not already placed in this home, why not and:
    - How often is visitation occurring and what is the impact on the child?
    - What is the detailed plan for the child's placement in this home and follow-up supervision after placement?
    - If a change of school will occur, what will be done to ease the transition?

Findings and Conclusions:

- Record the persons present and whether absent parties were provided with appropriate notice; verification that reports offered into evidence have been provided to all parties in advance of the hearing.
- A finding as to what reasonable efforts the agency has made to reunify the family and to finalize a permanent plan. A well-designed, appropriate case plan and meaningful case reviews should prevent unexpected findings of "no reasonable efforts" at this stage of a case. Should it be found that additional remedial steps are necessary, specific expectations should be set out in a detailed order, with a short

time frame (e.g., 30 days) for holding the follow-up permanency hearing. A copy of the order should be forwarded to the head of the social services agency.

- A statement addressing special factors or conditions of the child that are identifi ed as special needs, what services are to be provided to address these needs, and who is responsible for providing the services.
- The court's determination of the permanent plan for the child and why the plan is in the best interests of the child. The order should state the steps to be taken and time lines for accomplishing the permanent goal. If the plan is reunification, the date for reunification should be stated.
- If the plan is termination of parental rights and the petition has not yet been filed, the order should state expected time frame for filing a petition for termination of parental rights that must be within 30 days. If the petition has been filed, the court should schedule pretrials, mediation, and trial dates.
- If the plan is termination of parental rights, and a parent wishes to relinquish parental rights at the permanency hearing, the court should be prepared to accept the relinquishment and include the relinquishment in the order.
- For any plan, next hearing date and purpose, unless all court and agency involvement is terminated (i.e., permanent guardianship, permanent custody, or reunification without protective supervision).

For Review Hearings that Follow Permanency Hearings or Termination of Parental Rights Hearings

If Reunification Is the Permanent Plan:

- What progress has been made on each of the issues that prevented implementation of this plan at the permanency hearing?
- How often is visitation occurring and what is the impact on the child and family?
- What is the date and detailed plan for the child's safe return home and follow-up supervision after family reunification?
- What are the plans to continue any necessary services to the child?
- What are the plans to continue any necessary services to the family?

- If a change of school will occur, what will be done to prepare for the transition?
- If the family has not made adequate progress to enable a safe return home, what alternate permanent plan is recommended and what are the steps and time frames for its implementation?

If Permanent Guardianship or Permanent Custody Is the Permanent Plan:

- What progress has been made on each of the issues that prevented implementation of this plan at the permanency hearing?
- What contact is occurring between the child and parents, siblings, other family members and tribal and clan members, if applicable, and is this contact working well for the child and all involved individuals?
- Has there been full disclosure regarding the child's background history and current or potential disabilities?
- What are the plans to continue any necessary services to the child? How will these services be funded after guardianship or custody has been granted?
- What is the plan for financial support from the biological parents?
- Is there any reason that permanent guardianship or permanent custody should not be granted today?
- If sufficient progress has not been made to enable the granting of permanent guardianship or permanent custody at this hearing, what alternate permanent plan is recommended and what are the steps and time frames for its implementation?

If Relative or Foster Home Adoption Is the Permanent Plan:

- What progress in approving the relative or foster home as the adoptive home has been made since the termination of parental rights hearing? If it is not yet approved, why not, what remains to be done, and when will it be approved?
- Has there been full disclosure regarding the child's history, and current or potential disabilities?
- If adoption with contact has been agreed upon, what contact is occurring between the child and parents, siblings, other family members, or tribal and clan members, if relevant, and is this contact working well for the child and all involved individuals?

- How soon can the adoption be finalized? What specific steps must occur and what is the time frame for each of the steps?
- Has the adoption assistance agreement been negotiated? If not, why not? Have all appropriate subsidies been identified and has all paperwork been completed with regard to these subsidies? Will services follow the family if they move out of State? Is the adopting family aware of the details of all appropriate subsidy issues?
- Has the relative or foster parent been made aware of ways to access needed services after the adoption is finalized? Has the relative or foster parent been given contacts for support groups or other adopting families who can serve as mentors and supports?

If an Adoptive Home Has Been Recruited Since the Last Hearing but the Child Has Not Yet Been Placed in the Home:

- A detailed description of the family and the neighborhood in which the family lives. Is there another person who spends significant time in the home, and if so, has this individual been interviewed for appropriateness?
- If the child is an Indian child, does the home meet the placement preferences listed in the Indian Child Welfare Act, and if not, why not? What efforts has the agency made to identify a placement under Indian Child Welfare Act?
- Has there been full disclosure to the adopting family of the child's circumstances, history, special needs, and potential disabilities?
- Have all available subsidies been identified and discussed with the adopting family?
- Is the adopting family aware of any adoption with contact agreement and are they accepting of the agreement?
- What is the visitation and placement plan and its time frame? If visits have begun, how are the child and the adopting family adjusting?
- If the home is out of State, have all regulations regarding the Interstate Compact for the Placement of Children and the Interstate Compact on Adoption and Medical Assistance been followed? Are there any known or anticipated issues relative to these compacts that may cause delays and if so, what is being done to resolve or avoid the delays?
- Has there been full disclosure regarding the child's history and current or potential disabilities?

- What are the plans to continue necessary services to the child? How will services be funded after guardianship custody has been granted?
- What is the plan for financial support from the biological parents?
- Is there any reason that permanent guardianship or permanent custody should not be granted today?
- If sufficient progress has not been made to enable the granting of permanent guardianship or permanent custody at this hearing, what alternate permanent plan is recommended and what are the steps and time frames for its implementation?

If the Child Has Been in the Adoptive Home Since the Last Hearing:

- What progress has been made since the last hearing toward finalization? When will finalization occur? What specific steps must occur and what are the time frames for each step?
- Have any new problems or issues occurred since the last hearing? What is the plan to address the problems or issues?
- If full disclosure regarding the child's history and current or potential disabilities had not yet occurred at the last hearing, has it now occurred?
- If adoption with contact has been agreed upon, what contact is occurring between the child and parents, siblings or other family members, and is this contact working well for the child and all involved individuals?
- Has the adoption assistance agreement been negotiated? If not, why not? Have all appropriate subsidies been identified and has all paperwork been completed with regard to these subsidies? Will services follow the family if they move out of state? Is the adopting family aware of the details of all appropriate subsidy issues?
- Has the adopting family been made aware of ways to access needed services after the adoption is finalized? Has the adopting family been given contacts for support groups or other adopting families who can serve as mentors and supports?

If the Agency Is Recruiting an Adoptive Home:

- What efforts have been made since the termination of parental rights hearing or last review hearing to identify potential adoptive homes both locally and in other jurisdictions?

- If the child is an Indian child, what efforts are being made to identify potential adoptive homes in the child's tribal community?
- What is the status of investigating adults with whom the child has or has had a positive relationship with regard to their potential to become adopting families?
- On what adoption exchanges and Internet sites is the child listed?
- How many potential families have expressed interest in the child and what is the status of investigating each family?
- What efforts are being made by the agency to comply with Indian Child Welfare Act placement preferences, if applicable?

If Another Plan Is the Permanent Plan:

- What progress has been made since the permanency hearing and is the existing permanent plan still in the child's best interests?
- Do the compelling reasons not to proceed with reunification, termination of parental rights, permanent guardianship, or permanent custody that existed at the permanency hearing still apply?
- If they do not, what is the new permanent plan and how is it in the child's best interests? What are the steps and time frames that have occurred, or still need to occur to fully implement this new plan?
- What is the frequency and duration of contact that is occurring between the child and parents, siblings, other family members, tribal or clan members, or other signifi cant adults? Is this contact working well for the child and all involved individuals?
- What is the plan to prepare the child for independent living?
- If a change of placement is planned:
    - Why is this change necessary and in the best interests of the child?
    - What is the plan for pre-placement visits? Have they begun and how is the child responding? What is the detailed plan for the child's placement in this home and follow-up supervision after placement?
    - If a change of school or service providers will occur, what will be done to ease the transition?

Findings and Conclusions:

- Who is present at the hearing and whether absent parties were provided with appropriate notice. If the child is an Indian child, the court should verify whether the child's tribe received notice and was offered an opportunity to participate. It should be verified that reports provided to the court were made available to all parties prior to the hearing.
- A finding as to whether the agency has made reasonable efforts to finalize a permanent home with detail to support the finding. If the child is in an adoptive home, the finding should indicate whether the agency is doing everything possible, as quickly as possible, to approve the home, complete all aspects of the adoption assistance agreement including subsidies and services, and move toward finalization. If an adoptive home must be recruited, the finding should indicate whether the agency is doing everything possible, as quickly as possible, to list the child on all appropriate exchanges, Internet sites, and with all appropriate private agencies, and to promptly screen and complete home studies on prospective adopting parents.
- If the child is an Indian child, a finding as to whether the agency has complied with the placement preferences within the Indian Child Welfare Act, and if not, the efforts made to comply.
- If there are any changes or adjustments to the permanent plan, a description with time lines for implementation and the reasons that these adjustments or changes are in the best interests of the child.
- If visitation issues, including agreements for adoption with contact apply, are the terms and schedules of visitation being complied with and are they effective.
- A statement addressing special factors or conditions of the child that are identified as special needs, what services are being provided to address the needs and how the child is progressing.
- Any specific orders that are to be implemented.
- Unless the permanent plan is finalized at the hearing, the date and time for the next review or the finalization hearing.

Source: National Council of Juvenile and Family Court Judges. (2000). Adoptions and permanency guidelines: Improving court practice in child abuse and neglect cases. Reno, NV: Author.

APPENDIX E- LEGAL AND JUDICIAL ISSUES SUGGESTED BY THE CHILD AND FAMILY SERVICES REVIEW PERFORMANCE INDICATORS

To help States consider the legal dimensions of the seven safety, permanency, and well-being outcomes and the seven systemic factors (including the 45 related specific performance indicators identifi ed by the Federal government), this appendix annotates the 45 performance indicators addressed in the fi rst round of reviews. That is, the 45 Federal performance indicators are listed verbatim and boldface below, while legal and judicial aspects of each performance area are provided as bullets. *Note*: These bullets are meant to illustrate the kinds of legal practice and policy issues that may require attention to comply with each performance area.

I. SAFETY

1. **Timeliness in initiating child abuse and neglect investigations.**
   - Effective legal help is available to overcome barriers to investigations.
   - Legal advice is provided to the agency that supports the filing of actions in dependency court whenever abused and neglected children need State intervention.

- Legislation and court rules provide legal remedies allowing agencies to complete investigations when family members or other people familiar with the child refuse to cooperate.
- Statutes, regulations, and procedures provide clear and appropriate guidance for investigators and caseworkers to obtain otherwise confidential information from substance abuse treatment providers, criminal justice agencies, schools, mental health providers, doctors, and other professionals.

2. Recurrence of abuse or neglect by parents.

- Courts remove children from home and enforce comprehensive judicial protective supervision.
- Courts carefully consider safety factors when deciding whether to return a child home.
- Courts exercise caution when deciding whether to terminate court jurisdiction (dismiss case).
- Judges and attorneys take time to carefully review documents and ask challenging questions concerning safety issues in the home.
- Adequate evidence demonstrating danger to the child is offered in court proceedings.
- Judges carefully consider evidence about the child and caretakers to ensure the child will be safe.
- Domestic violence policies are well defined.

3. Services to protect children at home and prevent removal.

- In appropriate circumstances judges order parents to participate in services to protect the child instead of ordering the child removed from home.
- Adequate evidence demonstrating whether services will alleviate danger to the child is offered in court proceedings.
- Laws and regulations define an array of services for abused and neglected children and their families, to be delivered immediately in emergencies.
- Domestic violence policies are well defined.

4. **Risk of harm to child including abuse or neglect of child while in foster care.**
   - Courts order removal of children from their foster homes when the agency appropriately requests it to avoid potential abuse or neglect. (Note that courts do not have the power in all States to block removal of a child from a foster home.)
   - Courts monitor foster placements by insisting caseworkers and children's legal representatives visit and evaluate the foster home.
   - Safety clearances are done on every adult in the foster parents' or adoptive parents' homes.

Note: Many organizational problems may affect the factors listed below. Important examples are excessive workloads, insufficient training, poor hiring practices and management, and weak case management skills. These are common problems facing caseworkers, attorneys, foster parents, child advocates, judges, and court staff and can weaken the legal system.

II. Permanency

5. **Foster care reentry.**
   - Adequate time and resources are allocated for meaningful case review before sending the child home.
   - Courts require evidence that the home is safe before authorizing the child's return home.
   - When courts allow children to remain home following adjudication of child abuse or neglect, they require that the case be brought back to court if the agency decides to place the child in foster care. Due process protections regarding subsequent removal of the child are in place.
   - Courts order specific services and refer parents to community supports to make the return successful and require that parents and children complete the services.
   - Courts gather enough information about the parent and child before return.
   - Courts ensure visitation plans are designed to foster healthy parent-child relationships and work toward successful reunification to avoid foster care reentry (e.g., efforts are made to

ensure visits are meaningful, progressively longer visits are imposed).

- Courts and agencies closely monitor cases.
- Courts carefully and thoroughly consider the evidence when deciding whether to return children home.

6. **Stability of foster placement – too many moves of foster children into different foster homes.**
   - Judges monitor moves while children are in foster care.
   - Laws, regulations, and State policies discourage moving children between foster homes.
   - Policies and practices support training for foster parents of special needs children.
   - Judges understand bonding and attachment issues and factor them into decision-making.
   - Courts thoroughly review children's needs.
   - Children's counsel effectively represents children by:
     - Reviewing case plans;
     - Participating in case planning;
     - Preserving placements;
     - Advocating for reunification services;
     - Advocating for independent living services;
     - Visiting and interacting with the child to independently assess whether moves are necessary.

7. **Permanency goal for child.**
   - Attorneys, judges, and court personnel are adequately trained in permanency planning practices.
   - Permanency hearings are conducted in a timely manner and sufficient time is allotted for hearings.
   - Judges and attorneys understand concurrent planning and support it when appropriate.
   - State laws provide appropriate grounds for legal guardianship, clear and efficient procedures for establishing legal guardianships, and adequate legal protections and financial supports for legal guardians.
   - State laws provide appropriate grounds for termination of parental rights (TPR) and clear and efficient procedures for TPR.

- State laws and policies provide appropriate exceptions for mandatory petitions for TPR, based on Federal requirements.
- State laws and policies provide workable procedures for determining whether to file or join petitions for the TPR.

8. Reunification, guardianship, or permanent placement with relatives.

- Courts consistently follow or enforce time limits for hearings and judicial decisions. Courts have a comprehensive system of time limits governing all stages of the court process.
- Adequate judicial case tracking systems are in place.
- Judges fully explore all possible placement resources.
- Judges routinely establish or approve specific permanency plans for foster children.
- Courts minimize delays by notifying appropriate parties, denying adjournments, ensuring diligent efforts to locate missing parents at start of case, determining paternity early in case, and addressing other procedural problems.
- Multi-court involvement in different stages of child protection cases is discouraged to avoid delays, loss of information, and other inefficiencies.
- Court practices are efficient to minimize time to achieve reunification.
- Clear, efficient procedures exist to indefinitely transfer custody to a non-custodial parent or relative in child protection proceedings.
- State laws provide appropriate grounds for legal guardianship, clear and efficient procedures for establishing legal guardianships, and adequate legal protections and financial supports for legal guardians.
- Courts consistently and thoroughly review reasonable efforts to achieve a new permanent home for the child.

9. Achievement of adoption.

- Courts adequately track case progress toward adoption.
- Courts thoroughly consider the appropriateness of prospective adoptive caretakers.
- Judges fully explore all possible placement resources.

- Courts understand when TPR petitions are required and the exceptions to such requirements.
- Courts take steps to encourage or require TPR petitions, when appropriate.
- State laws provide appropriate grounds for TPR and clear and efficient procedures for TPR.
- Sufficient resources and court time are available to promote timely TPRs.
- The appellate process is streamlined to avoid TPR delays.
- Courts and attorneys inform agencies of available steps to speed appeals.
- Courts actively oversee cases between TPR and finalization of adoption
- Courts minimize scheduling delays and prioritize cases when needed.
- Courts minimize delays by notifying appropriate parties, denying adjournments, ensuring diligent efforts to locate missing parents at start of case, determining paternity early in case, and addressing other procedural problems.
- Multi-court involvement in different stages of child protection cases is discouraged to avoid delays, loss of information, and other inefficiencies.

10. Permanency goal of other planned permanent living arrangement.

- "Another planned permanent living arrangement" is clearly defined to avoid misapplication.
- Courts carefully use this permanency option, ensuring compelling reasons exist and giving thought to long-term permanency planning.
- Courts order or recommend services that might allow the child to move into a more permanent placement.
- Courts review case plans to determine agency compliance with services and visitation for other planned permanent living arrangements.
- Courts operate with the understanding that independent living (foster children "aging out") is not a permanency plan, but foster children are entitled to independent living services.

- Courts are familiar with available independent living services for children in the community and refer children to appropriate services.
- Courts are familiar with Federal legislation supporting independent living services.
- Courts ask about independent living services in most cases involving older teens in foster care.
- State laws authorize extending court jurisdiction for children who have turned 18 and specify appropriately.

11. Proximity of foster care placement.

- Courts request information about the proximity of the foster care placement.
- Courts do not order children placed outside their communities or counties if appropriate placement resources are located in close proximity.
- Courts routinely request information based on agency visits with children placed out of State.
- Statutes, court rules, and policies provide appropriate guidance concerning the proximity of foster care placement.

12. Placement with siblings.

- Courts consistently ask agencies to present specific reasons for failing to place siblings together.
- State statutes, court rules, and polices address the priority of placement with siblings.
- Attorneys and judges are adequately trained on the importance of maintaining sibling ties as well as on reasons why this might not be appropriate.

13. Visits with parents and siblings.

- Courts request information about the nature and quality of foster children's visits, contacts, and relationships with parents and siblings.
- Courts address visiting, when appropriate, in court orders.
- Attorneys request evaluations of the quality of visits with parents and siblings.

- Statutes, court rules, and policies provide clear guidance regarding visitation.
- Attorneys and judges are adequately trained on visitation issues.

14. Preserving connections.

- Attorneys request evaluations of relatives.
- Statutes, court rules, and policies provide clear guidance regarding maintaining relative ties.
- Attorneys are adequately trained on the importance and pitfalls of maintaining relative ties.
- Courts ask whether children are Native American and, if so, whether tribes have been notified.
- Courts support collaboration with tribal courts on transfers of cases of Native American children where appropriate.
- Courts enforce placement preferences for Native American children under ICWA, including placement with the child's extended family and with tribes.

15. Relative placement.

- Courts ask about possible placement with maternal and paternal relatives early and often.
- Courts ask agencies to present specific reasons for not placing children with relatives.
- Attorneys and judges are adequately trained on relative placement issues.

16. Relationship of child in care with parents.

- Courts consistently ask about child's relationship with parents while in care, including nature and quality of visits and other contact.
- Courts monitor visiting arrangements and their frequency where specified in court orders.
- Attorneys are adequately trained regarding maintaining parent-child relationships during foster placements.

III. Child and Family Well-Being

17. Needs and services of child, parents, foster parents.

- Courts ensure that agencies conduct thorough assessments and provide services to meet the needs of the child, parents, and foster parents.
- Courts review case plans submitted to the courts by the child protection agency to see if needs are being met through the provision of services.
- Courts address barriers to service provision and delivery.
- Attorneys and advocates identify and address their clients' needs and advocate appropriate services.
- Attorneys, advocates, and judges have sufficient training, experience, and resources to advocate effectively for children's service needs (e.g., special education, medical, and mental health needs).
- Judges and attorneys are sufficiently knowledgeable about confidentiality laws to help ensure that information on children's and family's needs is available to the court and agency.

18. Child and family involvement in case planning.

- Attorneys and advocates participate in and encourage child and family involvement in case planning.
- Statutes, court rules, and policies provide appropriate guidance to encourage child and family involvement in case planning.

19. Worker visits with the child.

- Statutes, court rules, and policies provide appropriate guidance on worker visits with parents and children.
- Attorneys and advocates request information about and, when appropriate, advocate for worker visits with the child.

20. Worker visits with parents.

- Courts consistently review and note worker visits with parents and children.
- Statutes, court rules and policies provide appropriate guidance on and, when appropriate, advocate for worker visits with parents.

21. Educational needs of the child.

- Courts request information about foster children's education from teachers, guidance counselors, caseworkers, and others.
- Court forms request education information including school records addressing the child's academic performance, behavior and adjustment to school, and special educational needs.
- Judges, attorneys, and advocates consistently determine whether foster children's education needs are being met.
- Policies offer guidance on minimizing disruptions in foster children's education due to frequent moves.
- State laws appropriately address confidentiality issues surrounding access to education records of foster children and children under protective supervision.
- Judges, attorneys, and advocates have sufficient knowledge about the education system to intervene effectively to ensure a good education for foster children.

22. Physical health of the child.

- Courts obtain information about foster children's medical needs.
- Court forms request physical health information, including any known medical problems, needed treatments, medication, and physical symptoms of abuse or neglect.
- Judges, attorneys and advocates consistently determine whether foster children's physical health needs are being met.
- Courts are aware of State requirements regarding foster children's physical health, such as those concerning medical examinations and immunizations.
- Courts inquire, when appropriate, whether health records have been reviewed, updated, and supplied to the foster care provider.
- State laws appropriately address confidentiality issues governing access to medical information about abused and neglected children.

23. Mental health of the child.

- Judges, attorneys, and advocates request information from children's therapists about foster children's mental health issues.
- Court forms request mental health information.

- Courts are aware of State requirements for diagnosis and treatment regarding foster children's mental health.
- Judges, attorneys, and advocates consistently determine whether foster children's mental health needs are being met.
- State laws appropriately address confidentiality issues governing access to mental health information.

IV. Statewide Information System

24. State operates information system that readily can identify the status, demographic characteristics, location, and goals for the placement of every child who is (or within the preceding year was) in foster care.

- Courts have created a statewide information system or good local information systems.
- Case tracking responsibilities are clearly assigned to appropriate court staff .
- Courts and agencies have automated systems that use computers and tickler systems to manage cases.
- Computer data is used to measure judicial performance.
- Agency information systems include information about critical court events to help evaluate judicial performance in child protection cases.
- Data are shared between judicial and agency computers.
- Sophisticated procedures exist to collect and report data.

V. Case Review System

25. Written case plan developed jointly with parents.

- Parents' attorneys participate in the case planning process.
- Parents' attorneys are trained on non-adversarial models for resolving conflict (i.e., Family Group Conferencing and mediation).
- Parents' attorneys advocate for meaningful case planning for their clients.
- Judges ask about parental involvement in case planning.

26. Process for periodic review at least once every six months, by court or by administrative review.

- Court procedures and forms ask hard questions and ensure thoroughness.
- Courts and/or agencies schedule 6-month reviews in a timely manner.
- Reviews thoroughly consider whether reasonable efforts have been made to achieve permanency, especially after the case goal is no longer reunification.
- Courts set aside enough time to hold review hearings that thoroughly consider the individual circumstances of each child and family and that address each issue specified by State and Federal law.
- If administrative reviews are held in lieu of judicial reviews, the courts take time to examine the reports from the reviews and address them in court proceedings.

27. Permanency hearings within 12 months after a child is considered to have entered foster care and at least once every 12 months thereafter.

- Adequate scheduling procedures for reviews are in place.
- Courts devote enough time to conduct thorough permanency hearings that address each issue specified in State and Federal statutes and to determine an appropriate permanency plan for each child.
- State laws, court rules, court forms, and court procedures create a structure for permanency hearings that encourages timely decisions by the court and agency, even in challenging cases.
- Permanency hearings thoroughly consider whether reasonable efforts have been made to achieve permanency, especially after the case goal no longer is reunification.

28. Process for termination of parental rights proceedings in accordance with ASFA.

- Attorneys and judges are aware of State and Federal statutory requirements to file petitions for TPR and of the exceptions.
- Courts routinely review agency documentation of exceptions to State and Federal requirements to file petitions for TPR.

- Procedures for TPR fully protect parents' rights without being needlessly inefficient.
- State laws do not require parties to reprove facts established in earlier stages of the court process in order to terminate parental rights.
- Grounds for TPR are complete, focused, and consistent.
- Agency procedures and policies for deciding whether to file are timely and balanced.

29. Process for foster parents, pre-adoptive parents, and relative caregivers of children in foster care to be notified of, and have an opportunity to be heard in, any review or hearing held with respect to the child.

- Courts consistently encourage active participation of foster parents, preadoptive parents, and relative caregivers in court proceedings.
- Foster parents, preadoptive parents, and relative caregivers consistently receive notice of court proceedings.
- The wording of notice forms encourages the attendance of foster parents, preadoptive parents, and relative caregivers in court.
- State laws and procedures specify an effective notification method for foster parents, preadoptive parents, and relative caregivers and define what is meant by "opportunity to be heard."
- Courts have forms and procedures for review and permanency hearings that call for statements by and questioning of foster parents, preadoptive parents, and relative caregivers.
- State laws and procedures clearly define an effective notification method for foster parents, preadoptive parents, and relative caregivers and define what is meant by "opportunity to be heard."
- State laws, court rules, and policies clarify and reinforce the role of foster parents, preadoptive parents, and relative caretakers in court.

VI. Quality Assurance System

30. Implementation of standards for services to children in foster care, to protect their health and safety.

- The agency has comprehensive standards for services to children in child protection cases and courts are aware of these standards.
- Agencies and courts work together to exchange information on services to children.

31. Quality assurance system in place to evaluate the quality of services, identify strengths and needs of service delivery system, provide relevant reports, and evaluate implementation of program improvement measures.

- Agencies enlist courts to help evaluate caseworkers' performance in court.
- Courts have systematic quality assurance systems to evaluate their own performance.

VII. TRAINING

32. Staff development and training program for all staff, including training on objectives of Title IV-B plan and services under Title IV-B and IV-E. To include initial training for all staff.

- The State agency provides copies of its Title IV-B and IV-E plans to all judges.
- The State agency provides to all judges and attorneys copies of lists of the services provided under Titles IV-B and IV-E.
- Training is provided for all new judges and attorneys concerning Title IV-B and IV-E and participation is mandatory.
- Comprehensive training is provided for all new judges and attorneys concerning child welfare law and basic social work principles and participation is mandatory.

33. Staff development and training to address ongoing skills needed to implement Title IV-B plan.

- Periodic training on child protection cases is provided for experienced judges and attorneys and participation is mandatory.
- Judicial and attorney training requirements for child protection cases are rigorous.
- Training on permanency planning concepts and procedures is provided to ensure timely permanence.

- Courts and agencies use appropriate cross training—addressing issues of mutual concern—and avoid inappropriate use of cross training in lieu of training in core legal skills and knowledge.

34. Training for prospective foster parents, adoptive parents, and staff of facilities with children receiving foster care or adoption assistance under Title IV-E.

- Prospective foster parents receive training on the legal aspects of permanency planning, including t4e stages and purposes of the legal process.
- Foster parents receive training and materials on their rights and responsibilities in child welfare proceedings, including the right to be heard and to participate in the case.
- Prospective adoptive parents receive training concerning their legal responsibilities and about the legal process of adoption.
- Foster parents, prospective adoptive parents and agency staff receive training concerning legal protections (e.g., procedural rights, entitlements, contractual rights) regarding adoption assistance.

VIII. Service Array

35. State has array of services. The array of services assesses strengths and needs of children and families, determines other service needs, addresses needs of individual children and of families to create a safe home environment, enables children to remain at home when reasonable, and helps children in foster and adoptive placements achieve permanency.

- Child protection agencies inform courts of available services, who is eligible for different services, and usual waiting periods for services.
- State laws, regulations, and budgets provide for a core of services that are consistently available to abused and neglected children and their families.

36. The services in the array (listed in response to the above item) are accessible to families and children in all political jurisdictions covered in the State's Title IV-E plan.

- Contracts for services are well written and ensure availability of needed services.
- Agencies have master plans for contracts to ensure consistent availability of key services.
- State laws require other agencies to give priority to and ensure availability of services to clients served by the child protection agency and under court jurisdiction.

37. The services in the array can be individualized to meet the unique needs of children and families served by the agency.

- State laws and policies budget for child protection services based on documented need for such services.
- Agencies' contracts for services provide flexible services to meet material and special needs of children and families.

IX. Agency Responsiveness to the Community

38. Ongoing consultation with tribal representatives, consumers, service providers, foster care providers, the juvenile courts, and other public and private child and family serving agencies and includes the major concerns of these representatives in the goals and objectives of the Title IV-B plan.

- Courts regularly meet with the agency and meet with all of the child protection professionals listed above to work on mutual problems and improve working relationships.
- Judicial ethics clarify and encourage judicial outreach to the agency and community regarding child protection cases.

39. The agency develops, in consultation with these representatives, annual reports of progress and services delivered under the Title IV-B plan.

- The agency consults with legal system representatives concerning its annual reports, including allowing them to review draft reports in advance. Among other things, the agency asks for comments concerning service delivery.

40. The State's services under the Title IV-B plan are coordinated with services or benefits of other Federal or federally assisted programs serving the same population.

- The agency consults with legal system representatives specifically concerning the delivery of federally assisted services provided by agencies and entities not funded by the child protection agency.

XI. Foster and Adoptive Parent Licensing, Recruitment, and Retention

41. Implementation of standards for foster family homes and child care institutions, reasonably in accord with national standards.

- Courts have information about standards for foster and adoptive parents and concerning child care institutions.

42. Standards applied to all foster family homes and child caring institutions receiving title IV-E or IV-B funds.

- Courts are informed when foster family homes and child caring institutions no longer meet agency standards.

43. State complies with Federal requirements for criminal background checks and has a case planning process that addresses the safety of foster and adoptive placements.

- State law requires criminal record checks of parents found to have abused or neglected their children and of other people living in the households of abused and neglected children.
- State law requires criminal record checks of all adults in foster and adoptive homes.
- Courts or court forms ask about the criminal record of parents found to have abused or neglected their children and of other people living in the households of abused and neglected children.
- Attorneys and judges are aware of State and Federal statutory restrictions concerning the licensing of specific categories of convicted criminals as foster and adoptive parents.

44. **State has process for diligent recruitment of potential foster and adoptive families that refl ect the ethnic and racial diversity of children in the State for whom foster and adoptive homes are needed.**
    - Courts and attorneys are well informed about the process of recruiting, matching, screening and evaluating foster and adoptive families.
    - In case reviews in which the permanency plan is adoption and the child is not yet placed in a preadoptive home, judges and advocates ask about State efforts to recruit and arrange such a home.
    - When evaluating whether the State made reasonable efforts to fi nalize a child's permanency plan, judges and advocates consider, if relevant, the State's efforts to recruit, evaluate, and select adoptive parents for the child.

45. **State has a process for effective use of cross-jurisdictional resources to facilitate timely adoptive or permanent placements for waiting children.**
    - Courts receive technical assistance, materials, and training on interstate placements (and overcoming barriers to such placements), including implementation of the ICPC.
    - Judges and attorneys are familiar with the ICPC, interstate adoption assistance benefits, ICAMA, and other interstate placement benefits and requirements.
    - Judges, attorneys, and advocates consistently ask informed and penetrating questions when interstate placement or services are being considered.

Source: Hardin, M. (2002). *How and why to involve the courts in your Child and Family Services Review (CFSR): Suggestions for agency administrators* [On-line]. Available:]
http://www.abanet.org/child/courtimp.html.

INDEX